PEARLS
IN THE
RAIN

Ruth Seamands

BRISTOL
BOOKS
WILMORE, KY 40390

Pearls in the Rain
© 1988 by Ruth Seamands
Published by Bristol Books
First Printing, June, 1988

Library of Congress Card Number: 88-70637
ISBN: 0-917851-18-8
Recommended Dewey Decimal Classification: 813.52 or F

Bristol Books
An Imprint of Good News, A Forum for Scriptural Christianity, Inc.
308 East Main Street • Wilmore, Kentucky 40390

Lovingly dedicated to my mother,
whose name was Pearl—and who *was* one;
to my mother-in-law, who was a mother to me;
and to my daughter Sheila,
who lovingly criticized and suggested.

Contents

Chapter 1

"*N*o, I don't understand!" Dave Hanson leaned over the table and glared at her. "I don't get it. You've made plenty of friends here—good friends. You've got a college degree, and soon you'll be finished at the business school. You can get a job at a good salary and stay right here. Lexington, Kentucky, may not be the center of the world, but Australia must be the end of it." He paused, then asked, "Did you ever think about marrying me?"

"Of course! I've thought about it a lot. But," she teased him, "Oh, you know—you're the boss's son, and if you marry a trainer's daughter—"

He ignored the good-natured taunt. "Come off it! That's an ancient idea, Julia."

She traced a pattern on the place mat with her fork. "Dave, you know the answer. We like each other a lot. We've been good friends for a long time, but you're not in love with me. You don't do a double handspring when you see me, and I don't choke up when I see you."

"So, who wants Hollywood all the time?"

"But someday you *will* choke up over a girl, and I wouldn't want to be the third one in that triangle."

"Don't go back to Australia, Julia," he pleaded. "What's there that you can't find here? You don't even know the place anymore."

"You're probably right. Blame it on itchy feet, but I've been restless ever since Mother and Dad died last year. It's an elusive thing, Dave. I feel I ought to be doing something different and don't know what it is. So when this letter came from Aunt Rosa last week, I just felt that was it, at least for now. She's the only relative I have left, and I ought to see her. I *should* go home to Australia for a while."

Dave didn't give up easily. "Yes, go, and maybe you'll hate her. Old aunts can be a pain. Maybe she's a nut. Why isn't she married?"

"She's been married."

"Does she have any money? You don't need it."

"Oh, Dave! Of course it isn't her money. She's lonely maybe. My dad was her only brother. I remember her as sort of fluttery and fancy, and she always smelled good. I like people who smell good."

"You're a nut too. So she's 'fluttery and fancy'!"

Julia ignored him "I remember the last time I saw her, the day we left Australia. She was wearing a frilly, pink summer dress and a flowered hat with a wide, droopy brim. I looked over the rail of our ship and waved to her. She was waving a pink handkerchief in our direction, but she was smiling up at a tall, distinguished-looking man beside her. She always had lots of men friends. I had the feeling she'd already forgotten we were leaving. But I'm sure she's missed us."

"Are you sure you have enough money? Enough to take you to Australia and to last until you find a job?"

"Oh, yes, there is Dad's insurance. As soon as I finish the business courses, I'll visit Sydney and get a job there for a while. If I don't like it, I'll come back here. I really do love Lexington, but my roots are in Australia."

"Roots! You're more American now than you are Australian. Don't forget, you've been in Kentucky since you were 12."

"Yes," Julia grinned at him. "I'll never forget that first day we arrived at your farm. You were sitting astride the biggest horse I'd ever seen, and you offered to let me ride. I thought you were wearing shining armor, but it must have been only blue jeans."

"Yes, and you! You were all legs and red, chunky braids and long dresses—and that crazy Australian accent! I couldn't understand half the things you said. Now I understand what you say, but not the way your brain works."

"Remember," Julia asked, "when you taught me how to whistle for the horses? I envied you because you were such a great whistler."

"Yes, I remember. And when you learned it, your whistle was so loud and shrill that nobody could stand it! I don't see why the horses didn't run away!"

"They like it. All they did was twitch their ears and come when they heard my special version of your whistle." She touched his hand on the tablecloth. "I'll never forget our good times, Dave, or the horses or these rolling hills. Lexington must be the most beautiful spot in the world."

"Then stay here!"

"Dave, I'll never forget you. I really like you very much, and no one has been closer to me. But as I told you, something keeps urging me. It may sound silly, but it's as if I have some unusual destiny to fulfill. Do you ever feel like that?"

Dave shrugged. "No, I suppose I've always known my destiny would be here in the bluegrass country. I'll travel, of course, but—"

"Will you visit me in Australia sometime?"

"Probably. But I couldn't stay away from here. You can understand that, Julia. Your dad loved horses the way I do. That's why he came over to work on our farm in the first place. He just wanted to work with horses. That's my love too."

"I know." Julia leaned back and looked at the traffic moving down South Broadway without seeing it. She missed Dave and Lexington already. Still, she wanted to go. Ever since the car crash the year before, there had been the restless and rootless feeling. Maybe Sydney had an answer for her.

"Have you told your Sunday school class yet?"

"No. That's as tough as telling you. Those kids mean a lot to me. Some of those 13-year-olds receive enough love and respect at home, but some of them come to Sunday school just for a chance to express an opinion and not be laughed at. You wouldn't believe some of the discussions we get into during that class."

"Like what?"

"Like: Why shouldn't a guy wear an earring if he wants to? Like: What's wrong with using drugs if it makes you feel happy and sleepy and makes you love everybody? Like: Why does my mom ground me so much? Why won't she *listen* to me?" Julia caught her breath. "Sometimes I come from that class exhausted! I love those kids, but I'm not smart enough to answer all their questions."

Resigned to Julia's decision, Dave heaved a deep sigh. They left the restaurant and walked to his car in silence.

The weeks passed quickly and soon Julia's business classes ended and she earned the diploma qualifying her for a top secretarial position. She could work with numerous machines, and she also knew shorthand. She packed that diploma with the one from the University of Kentucky that was her proof she had graduated with a degree in elementary education. She had first thought of teaching. But when her parents died so suddenly, standing before a class of children all day long seemed impossible. So rather desperately she'd enrolled in the business school. Well, being qualified in two fields ought to make it easier to find something to do in Sydney.

There wasn't too much to pack—her books and clothes, blue ribbons and trophies for riding and jumping, her stereo and records. The house and furniture, of course, all belonged to Dave's father. They'd been living on his farm for 12 years. *I am now 24 years old—it's time to go.*

The next Sunday Julia told her class she was leaving. It was hard to do; genuine affection bound them. The girls seemed stunned for a moment then bombarded her with questions. "But Miss Harrell, will we ever see you again?"

"What's Australia like? Are there really lots of kangaroos?"

"What about the Australian bushmen? Are they dangerous?"

"But Miss Harrell, you make Sunday school fun. Most people don't make it interesting. It's just boring!"

There were tears of regret, some her own. She felt she'd made at least a small investment in their lives.

Friends gave her a boisterous dinner party at a motel and dunked her in the swimming pool as a parting gesture. Dave put on a big rescue act and swam around the pool, pulling her by her red hair. Then he wrapped a blanket around her and led her dripping and squishing through the lobby to his car.

"A wet farewell to Lexington," she managed through chattering teeth.

The next day she waited with her luggage for Dave to come and take her to Bluegrass Airport. Like a lost child she wandered through the house, tears of solitude burning her eyes and splashing down her blouse.

Recollections washed over her: her red-haired, plump, comfortable mother, and her pencil-slim, sandy-haired father with his deeply-lined, weathered face. She pictured the three of them eating at the small kitchen table. Her dad was reading the Bible, as he did every night. Julia was inhaling in ecstasy the aroma of hot bread. Talk of colts and training. Horses to them were people. The odor of harness polish. She was studying while Mother knitted. Mother was cutting off her long braids and crying. It was all there for a final reconnoiter.

But her childhood sanctuary was no longer hers. The furniture was nothing but furniture anymore, with no lingering personality of those who had used it so long. Without two knitting needles stuck into a fat ball of yarn, the corner of the couch was an overstuffed wasteland. Without Dad's jacket and cap, which smelled of horses, hanging beside the door, the back room was sterile and desolate.

The windows of her own room upstairs looked out upon a curving, white-fenced, green checkerboard, but she wasn't gamboling on the checkerboard anymore. It was just another Lexington horse farm. The fences—she'd climbed every square inch of that fence sometime or another, but that climbing wraith was gone. It was now time to abandon the silent cocoon, remote and impersonal, which no longer nourished her.

Chapter 2

*T*he big jet roared low over the red roofs of Sydney, settled down on the runway and taxied in the sunshine toward the terminal. Beyond the customs counter inside, Julia saw a lacy, white handkerchief fluttering beside an impeccably dressed gentleman.

Aunt Rosa.

She clasped Julia to her for a moment, then pushed her back for a clearer view. Julia was sure her aunt needed glasses to bring her face into focus. She smelled of exotic perfume and was neatly groomed with lighter hair than Julia had remembered. Aunt Rosa wore a flawless yellow silk suit, and her slightly aging skin glowed. She was still beautiful. Completely feminine. No wonder she always had an escort; she made men feel so needed and so totally masculine.

"My darling Julia! After all these years! Well, you aren't as big as I thought you'd be. This is Frederick"—waving her hand toward her companion—"you'll get used to seeing him." Without pausing for breath, "You've taken after your father, but with your mother's hair coloring. And such a beautiful color! You're very pretty. Isn't she, Frederick?"

Julia felt a rush of love for her aunt. "Oh, Aunt Rosa! You're just the way I remembered you—soft and sweet and smelling of my favorite perfume. Thank you for asking me to come back to Sydney. I've been so restless, I might have come back anyway, even if you hadn't asked me."

"Well, my dear, I live alone in a large house, as you know, and it will be fun to have you around."

They climbed into the latest model American car. It belonged to Frederick—Aunt Rosa's friends were never poor. Aunt Rosa chattered all the way to her house. "There are so many things to do in Sydney, I don't think you'll be at all bored. We have a marvelous opera house—wait until you see it—all wings and sails, it looks like a sailing ship. And we have a revolving restaurant from which, I declare, you can see all the way to New Zealand." Aunt Rosa burbled on, her silent companion unable to insert a word. Julia's head whirled with fatigue after so many hours of flying and with trying to follow Aunt Rosa's thoughts which jumped around like a kangaroo family in tall grass. Aunt Rosa hadn't changed a bit.

Several days passed before Julia's body was reoriented from jet lag. Days and nights seemed reversed. She wanted to sleep while everyone else was awake, and she wanted to go out and rediscover Sydney while everyone else was sleeping. She wondered how the airline pilots managed to fly to as many countries as they did and recuperate from jet lag so often.

But on the fourth morning Julia stretched like a warm cat in her soft bed. Aunt Rosa had given Julia a beautiful room—all white, graceful furniture, scalloped curtains and bed flounces, soft chairs before a fireplace—just the kind of room to relax in—and to smother in. Julia couldn't stay here always, nice as it was. Her life couldn't be that luxurious forever. She wondered what she should do first.

She flopped downstairs in robe and slippers and scanned job opportunities in the morning paper while drinking some coffee. Waitress? No. Ticket girl in a movie house? No. Typist in a lawyer's office? Sounded good. She could do that. Receptionist at King's Cross hotel desk? Meet a good many people that way. Tour guide on a city bus? She'd forgotten too much about Sydney. Saleslady in an import shop? A book shop? The list seemed endless.

She circled the lawyer and hotel possibilities, dressed carefully and took a taxi to the lawyer's office. Several girls were waiting. They stared covertly at each other. As they sat waiting, an office door opened and a portly, red-faced gentleman emerged. He thanked them all for coming in to answer the advertisement, and he said he was sorry to inconvenience them, but the position had been filled. Beyond his open door, Julia caught a glimpse of a well-formed leg, crossed and trailing a bright red shoe.

She scratched off the lawyer.

The hotel had not yet hired a receptionist. She talked to the manager and within a few minutes the job was hers! For the next three days she was supposed to watch and learn. The girl she would replace was soon moving away from Sydney with her new husband.

As Julia observed she digested their method of answering the phone and giving information. She received instruction on the operation of the switchboard, learned to put up the mail and record reservations, met the other employees and began to feel at home.

There was constant hubbub in the hotel lobby. People from everywhere whirled in and out. Teenage parties from Europe and America trooped through. Wrestling and football teams thundered through. Honeymoon couples and retired couples on second honeymoons held hands and wandered through. Elevators stuck, baggage was lost and recovered. Children wandered up and down halls on the wrong floors and calls from frantic mothers jammed the switchboard. Guests paid bills from fat wallets, and some left King's Cross without paying. The three girls at the desk were constantly on call for something. Taking care of the ever-increasing number of temporarily homeless people was, for a while, Julia's responsibility. The Bluegrass seemed far away, but sometimes a "Kentucky Wildcats" basketball sticker on a piece of luggage made her search the accompanying group for a friendly face. She was tired at night but felt constantly exhilarated, as if this were an interlude before destiny intervened.

One afternoon during a lull, one of the hotel guests leaned on the desk. "Good afternoon, Miss—" looking at the identification badge pinned to her blouse, "Harrell. My name is William Banner. Would you please check the entertainment list to see what is going on around here this afternoon?"

But when Julia gave him the list he only glanced at it. *Funny,* she thought, *but this wiry and energetic man seemed lonely, needing someone to talk to.* He was tall and rugged-looking, as if he spent a great deal of time outdoors. His light brown hair was streaked with lighter brown as if well acquainted with sunshine.

"Is this your first visit to Sydney?" Julia asked.

"Yes—for quite a while, it is. For the past three years I've been working in Papua New Guinea."

"I've heard New Guinea is a difficult country."

"You couldn't imagine just how difficult until you saw it. Where did you pick up that American accent? Are you an American?" William Banner smiled and his teeth were straight and white. His velvet brown eyes twinkled.

"Well, I was born here in Australia, but I lived in Lexington, Kentucky, in the States, for 12 years. While I was there, kids used to tease me about my 'Aussie' accent. They couldn't understand a word I said. My friends used to make me spell words; then they'd laugh and ask, 'Did you say A or I in the middle of that word?'"

They laughed together. Then William moved a little and leaned casually against the counter while Julia answered the phone. After she distributed some room keys and promised a guest she'd send up another television set while his broken one was being repaired, she leaned on the desk. "What is your job in New Guinea, Mr. Banner?"

"I'm in an engineering office in Port Moresby just now.

That's on the coast, but my work often takes me up into the highlands. That's where the going gets thorny at times." His eyes lit up with enthusiasm. "But if you like adventure and challenge, you should come to New Guinea." He grinned, showing those strong, white teeth in a weather-beaten bronzed face. "But no sissies invited!"

That piqued her curiosity. "But what could I *do* there?"

"There's plenty to be done because part of that country is still coming out of the Stone Age. Can you type, keep books, trek through a jungle, wade rivers, digest odd food, live with human weakness and love your neighbors? Can you live on sweet potatoes? Do you like pigs? If so, you'd probably fit into New Guinea. Can I bring you a cup of coffee?"

"I'm gasping after listening to that! Better make it strong."

He sprinted into the dining room and came back with two cups of coffee and some cookies on a tray. In between switchboard calls and other interruptions they drank their coffee, and he told her about New Guinea.

Julia sighed. "You make it sound so fascinating, my feet are itching!"

"But if you're allergic to cockroaches, leeches, cold houses, mildew, mud, jeeps, smelly pig grease or superstitious people, you'd better not go. You're bound to encounter all of them at one time or another, or maybe all at once."

"It certainly doesn't sound very tranquil."

"No, not tranquil. But once you got used to it, you'd love it as I do. A ruggedness and a challenge exist there that you won't find in Sydney. Look," he said, pulling a newspaper out of his pocket, "did you see this item in today's paper? This is our company." His finger traced a boxed article while a lock of light brown hair fell into his eyes.

"Secretaries wanted to fill engineering outposts. There is hardship, challenge and adventure for anyone brave enough to go to New Guinea. Inquire, Post Office Box AS 262."

"You would be helping to build a young nation," William said.

"So they really do need more company secretaries there?"

"They certainly do. Our company paper work comes through very slowly because in many outposts the administrator has to do his own typing. And most administrators only hunt and jab through most of their typed communications." He finished his coffee. "So if you're brave and healthy," he glanced at her ring finger, "not tied to Sydney, and if you type more than 25 words per minute, you could probably have the most exciting time of your life in New Guinea. You would have to sign up for a two-year stint at first, but after one year there, you'd get a month's leave back here in Australia. I've already had three years, and now I'm going back for another two years."

He looked at his watch. "Well, it's been a pleasure talking to you, Miss Harrell. I've promised to take my young niece out for a drive today, and tomorrow I must fly out. Thank you for allowing me to bore you about New Guinea. Goodbye."

"Goodbye, Mr. Banner. I wasn't at all bored!" What a happy dynamo, she thought, watching him leave the hotel.

William had forgotten his newspaper and several times that afternoon Julia stared down at the boxed item he had called to her attention. She slipped one shoe off and idly rubbed the sole of her freed foot on the top of her other shoe and reread the article: "Secretaries wanted to fill engineering outposts. There is hardship, challenge and adventure for anyone brave enough to go to New Guinea."

The element of "dare" intrigued her, and William had said, "no sissies invited!" She thought about William Banner and New Guinea all the rest of the day.

That night as she curled up in her thick, soft bed, she still thought of William Banner and his "cold houses, mildew, mud, smelly pig grease and superstitious people." Not that *she* would like to live in such a way! *Oh, well, it's good for the world that audacious people like Banner are willing to venture out and live in that kind of place.* Drowsily luxuriating in the smooth sheets and faintly perfumed pillows, she soon drifted off to sleep, scratching her left foot with her right big toe. She dreamed she was trekking through a jungle, carrying a sweet potato in her hand.

While sleeping, Julia made a subconscious decision. The next morning she thought, *Well, why not? I don't have to promise anything now, but it might be fun to check out the ad. Let's see, what was that address? I'd better not mention this to Aunt Rosa; I know what her reaction to smelly pig grease would be. Imagine Aunt Rosa in a place like that!*

She wrote a letter of inquiry and was called in for two interviews followed by a few days of mounting excitement. Then Julia, shocked at herself, signed a contract to work in New Guinea for two years of her life! And she'd never felt so alive!

In high spirits she burst into the house that afternoon. Aunt Rosa was lying back in a chaise lounge, her manicure equipment spread out on a small table beside her. Her eyes were covered with two, round, witch hazel pads. "Aunt Rosa, guess what! I'm going to New Guinea to work as a secretary for an engineering company!"

Aunt Rosa jerked up, bewildered, eye pads plopping into her chiffon lap. Her eyes grew round. "Why, Julia, dear, whatever for? Aren't you happy here? I like having you here."

Julia sat at the foot of the chaise lounge. "I know I should have mentioned it before, but I just wasn't sure about my own feelings. Of course I'm happy here, Aunt Rosa. It isn't that. I just have a feeling, an urge, that this is the thing toward which I've been moving for a long time. It's almost like destiny calling. I know it sounds crazy."

"But Julia! New Guinea? It's a horrible country." Aunt Rosa's chin trembled."

"Oh, Aunt Rosa, don't worry. I know it's a hard place in which to live, but it's a real challenge, a place to prove to myself I can get along in hard places. I've always had life so easy."

"But that's the way life should be! Happy! Not all rough and scratchy, harsh walking shoes and coarse dresses! How could you be feminine in such a place?"

"Few women can be as feminine as you, Aunt Rosa, no matter how they try or where they are."

Aunt Rosa blinked wide, tearful blue eyes. "Julia, surely you don't intend going there! That country is still in the Dark Ages. Why, you might come down with some kind of weird disease, or even be eaten by cannibals! Oh—there's the bell, and my nail polish isn't dry. Do let Frederick in and talk to him please!" Aunt Rosa fluttered into her dressing room and that was the extent of her objections to Julia's outlandish itinerary.

Chapter 3

*R*ugged peaks thrust dark, spiked ridges toward the sky. Waterfalls were slender threads when viewed from the air. A few thatched roofs here and there clung to the mountainsides. After flying in a Trans-Australian Air Lines jet from Sydney to Port Moresby on the south coast of New Guinea, this small Papuan Air Lines plane seemed too fragile to fly 11,000 feet over such mountains.

The plane tilted and Julia gasped. The wings were almost touching steep slopes on both sides as the tiny plane circled deep inside a ring of peaks before touching down on the valley floor. A slender, long house straddling a ridge halfway up a jungle-covered slope, a small settlement surrounding a narrow, white airstrip on the valley floor—this was Bulai. Bulai in Papua New Guinea.

Her supervisor, in charge of the engineering crew for the Bulai area, was there to meet her. A girl about Julia's age stood beside him. "I am Grant Richards, Miss Harrell. Welcome! We need you here and hope you will be happy. This is Miss Mary Day who works in our office. You will share a company house with her."

She shook hands with Grant and smiled. He was not very tall, had a rather round figure, and his hair was as bright red as her own. She just had to grin. "Anybody with hair that color has to be okay!" Then she turned to greet Mary.

"How do you do, Julia. Welcome to Bulai," Mary said.

Grant looked beyond her. "Hello! There's William Banner. I knew he'd be around to meet my new secretary!"

William, about six-feet-one, climbed out of a Land Rover. "Good morning, Grant. She came, I see." He smiled down at Julia. "She's pretty too!"

Julia gasped as her mouth dropped open. Didn't he remember her?

"Might as well get this over with," Grant grumbled. "Miss Harrell, may I present William Banner. Watch him; he's a terror with the ladies. He hasn't been here very long, but I've been observant."

Julia kept a straight face. "How do you do, Mr. Terror."

Then they both burst out laughing.

Grant looked startled. "I say, Banner, do you already know each other?"

William tried to keep from smiling. "I'll have to confess now. When Miss Harrell's acceptance and assignment papers came through the Port Moresby office, I noted she would be in your office. So I asked to be transferred to your area. I was afraid to tell you why I made that request. I was afraid you'd kick me out!"

"Well, Banner," Grant growled, "if I didn't need you so much around here, I'd still kick you out!"

William grinned at Julia. "Since I was the one who told Miss Harrell about New Guinea in the first place, I thought it my duty to, sort of, be here to help her get adjusted."

"When duty and pleasure don't clash, let everything else go to smash, or something like that," Grant mumbled. "It's a quote, I think, or maybe I made it up on the spur of the moment. Okay, Banner, you'll have to work twice as hard for this deception." Then Julia saw his eyes twinkle. "But not today."

Grant picked up Julia's large piece of luggage while they got into the Land Rover. "You've arrived at a colorful time, Miss Harrell. This native gathering happens once a week."

It was market day, and from the airstrip she could see people walking leisurely from all directions toward a large open space, about three acres in extent. A small wood-and-corrugated metal building which served as the airport office bordered the area. Most people were barefoot, with dark brown, shiny bodies adorned with the least possible clothing. The men wore wide belts of brown bark, with a little black netting in front and a few green leaves in back. The women wore only beige-colored grass skirts. Everyone had on some kind of lustrous pearl-shell necklace.

Several women were thickly encrusted with gray clay over their whole bodies. Even their faces and eyelids were covered with clay, giving them a ghostly masked appearance. Their eyelids were so weighed down the women peered out from mere slits. Numerous strands of small, grey beads encircled their necks, heavily cascading over bare breasts to their waists. Some women carried pigs in their arms and babies in net bags slung from their foreheads and down their backs. One man had quite a large pig hoisted over his shoulder.

Julia wanted to know everything at once. "Why is that woman carrying a *pig*? Why is that lady dressed with all those beads and grey mud? Is that supposed to be a beauty pack? What is the black stuff all over that young girl? It looks like axle grease."

William laughed. "You'll get used to it all. The lady in clay and beads is in mourning. Those beads are called 'Job's tears.' Sometimes they wear as much as fifteen pounds of them. Those people are carrying pigs because pigs are precious here. When there's nobody at home to look after their pigs, they take them along wherever they go. The black grease shows that the other young lady has just been married. It's the custom among these people that, right after a marriage ceremony, the bride is smeared with that mixture of charcoal and oil. She can't go and live with her husband until it wears off."

"He probably wouldn't want to live with her like that anyway! How long will it take to wear off?"

"Usually a couple of months. But some of the smart young village men have found out about soap and water!"

"What a way to spend a honeymoon," Julia murmured, "all smeared up with oil and charcoal!"

The Land Rover bumped up a narrow road to a small house set on a hill. They all climbed out and the two men took Julia's luggage inside. Grant turned to her, "No work today, Miss Harrell. Let William show you all around Bulai. It seems he's been waiting three weeks to do that very thing."

"You've just told me to watch out for him because he's a terror with the ladies, and now you're turning me over to him?"

"You couldn't be in better hands. He'll show you where our office is."

"It would probably be a good idea for you to wear some comfortable walking shoes, Miss Harrell." William glanced at her dressy shoes. "Some places are rough. And it begins to get cooler in the afternoons, so bring a jacket."

She spent the rest of the day with William, exploring the small settlement of Bulai in his Land Rover. There wasn't much to see: a few government buildings of wood with corrugated-metal roofs; homes perched on the hillsides, some built of wood and some of woven mats. He pointed out a cluster of buildings at one end of the Bulai road, which was an Australian mission station. One of the buildings, a large, metal-sided structure with wide doors, was filled with all kinds of sturdy vehicles: jeeps, station wagons, Land Rovers and trucks. No fancy cars with comfortable seats. Two young men working on a jacked-up Land Rover smiled and waved as they passed.

"Those two can fix anything that runs on wheels or that has any kind of motor," William said, nodding toward the men. "They keep not only their own vehicles repaired but also those owned by the government and ours, too. I don't know

what we'd do if there were no mission station here. We'd
have to bring out our own mechanics. Of course we do simple
repairs for the Land Rovers ourselves, but they do the heavy
stuff for us."

"Have these mechanics been here very long?"

"No, only about a year. But things literally began to move
after they arrived. Marvin, the thin one with light hair, is dat-
ing Mary Day—the girl you'll be living with."

"How many people are located at this mission station?"

"There are three couples, three single girls and six single
men. Oh, yes, also five children. The bishop and his wife have
three children and his helper has two. The other couple has
none. The men, that is, the single men, all work on construc-
tion. They built this road, put in the electrical system you see
there," he pointed to poles and wires strung from house to
house," and installed a dam and water system. The work is
hard and tiring, but they don't seem to mind the hardship at
all. They are dedicated people and have accomplished much
in the few years they have been here."

"What do the girls do?"

"The married one who has no children and two of the
single girls are teachers. The other single girl acts as secretary
for everybody else."

"What's the school like?"

"Well, the girls studied Bulai language and are now teaching the Bulai children English. But they had to study Bulai
first, so they could understand the children. Some of the
teenagers and even a few of the adults from the nearby village are also going to the mission school to learn English. Do
you know any pidgin?"

Julia shook her head. "No, but I've heard about it. Sounds
like a grand corruption of English, doesn't it? I've heard it's
a laughable language."

"Yes, it's a corruption of English with other foreign words
tossed in. Some of their expressions are funny, but enough

like English to be partly understandable to the beginner. It's the trade language here in New Guinea."

"Is there any literature in pidgin?"

"Yes, some. The Bible has been translated into it, some pamphlets and songs."

"Then why not teach everybody English, so the people will have a lot to read?"

"That sounds much more simple than it really is. But someday it may happen."

"What is your job here, Mr. Banner?"

"William, please."

"Not Bill?"

"No, that's too American."

"All right, William, what are you doing driving new secretaries around all day in the hills of Papua New Guinea?"

"May I call you Julia?"

"Please do."

"Having the time of my life, Julia." He said grinning. "Your coming is the best thing that's happened around here in ages! But as to my work, I had a degree in mines and minerals, worked for a while in Australia, then thought I would explore what I could do in New Guinea. I love it here. It's a challenge."

"Mines and minerals? Are you digging for something special here?"

"I had hoped to find some gold in this area, but so far I haven't found any. So I'm helping the Agriculture Department with experiments on how to improve the copra production and various other things. One of them is a plant which furnishes a potent drug."

William took her over incredible roads—not roads, really. They were narrow, full of rocks, up hills and around sharp curves, with miniature bridges spanning mountain streams. Ragged jungles marched uphill alongside. At one small bridge some of the rough planks were missing, having fallen about 10 feet below into the stream.

Some small, naked boys were walking along the road by the bridge just as the Land Rover came to a halt. William smiled at them and called out a question completely unintelligible to Julia. The boys grinned widely, scrambled down the slope into the stream, and one by one carried up the missing log pieces for the bridge. When the last one was in place, William fished around in his pocket and brought out some gum—giving a stick to each boy. They ran off happily, their wet, naked bodies glistening, their cheeks bulging.

"Where did you get that gum, way out here?" Julia had been sitting on a rock by the stream watching the little boys and enjoying a view of steep slopes beyond the river. There was a never-ending panorama of light and shadow as incredibly white, fluffy clouds floated over the mountain, alternately obscuring the sun.

"While I was in Sydney, I stocked up on many unusual items like gum, beads, umbrellas, small bags and so forth. They'll all come in handy here. We all bring out gum and small things to give as gifts at Christmastime. The news spread around about what to do with the gum. They'll chew it for a month; then they will probably put it up in their hair to help achieve some new style!"

She laughed as he helped her back into the Land Rover. He was such fun to be with, so easy to talk to. They bumped slowly over the newly repaired bridge, and she held her breath. It was rickety and shook and swayed as they drove over. Maybe some day she'd get used to such bridges.

They passed many people walking along the narrow road, all going home from market day in Bulai. They were carrying an assortment of sweet potatoes, nuts, bananas, pigs and babies. When the Land Rover overtook them, they stepped aside, smiled and waved.

"They seem to be friendly. Tell me more about these people. Tell me everything you know about them," Julia urged.

"Well, that will take a little more than one afternoon.

Maybe if I spin it out into a long tale, I'll have a chance to see you often." His brown eyes crinkled at the corners.

"Great! You can be my teacher." He didn't seem at all lonely here, as he had when she saw him in Sydney. Here he was relaxed and perfectly at ease. There was a comfortable silence.

He smiled at her. "Julia, I hope you didn't mind finding me here when you arrived in New Guinea. When I met you in Sydney, I mourned over the fact that we had no time to get acquainted. And when I told you about New Guinea you seemed so interested. I hoped you would come and I yelled like a happy kid when I heard you were. What made you decide to come?"

"My feet kept itching."

He threw back his head and laughed.

"Really!" she insisted. "My feet always itch when I'm supposed to do something different. They itched when I was in America and was supposed to come to Sydney. I think Mother Nature hooked radar between my feet and destiny. Now stop laughing! After you told me about New Guinea, I was forever having to take off my shoes to scratch my feet. It was a little annoying when I was trying to help a hotel guest. And every night I went to sleep scraping one foot with the other big toe."

He gave in to loud guffaws and when he regained his composure, he asked, "Feet itching anymore?"

"Not a tingle!"

"Maybe I misjudged you. You might be a little crazy after all!"

He pulled over to the side of the road. "Feel like climbing a little? I'll take you to a favorite spot of mine." He pointed to a hill whose slope looked gentle enough to climb easily. "See up there, about three-quarters of the way, that dark spot? It isn't really hard to get to, and the view is worth every minute of the climb."

They started climbing the hill, but after five minutes Julia stopped, puffing. "Let me get my breath. This is harder than it looked!"

"It's the altitude," he sympathized. "It gets everyone at first, but after a few weeks here you'll probably beat me to the top." He paused. "Did you like living in the U.S.A.? I hope to go to America someday. How did you happen to live there?"

"Well, when I was 11 years old a Mr. Hanson came to Australia as a tourist. He owned a big horse farm in Kentucky, and he was traveling out in the bush country looking at our Australian breeds. My father was working with horses, the great love of his life. Mr. Hanson liked Dad and appreciated the way he handled the animals, so he invited him to go to America and work for him. I was 12 when we arrived there. It was all very exciting."

"Once you got settled there, did you like it?"

"I loved it. The bluegrass region of Kentucky is perfectly beautiful. The hills are not rugged or peaked like these. There it's just soft, green, rolling hills with white fences and sleek, powerful horses."

"You sound a little homesick. Any loves left in America?"

"No, only the boy next door, Mr. Hanson's son, Dave. And he's almost like my brother."

They began to climb more slowly now. Julia continued, her voice catching, "Mother and Dad were killed in a car crash last year."

William pressed her arm in sympathy.

"After that I felt restless and had to do something. I had a degree in elementary education and intended to teach. But I just couldn't bring myself to stand in front of a class all day long so soon after my parents' death. So I enrolled in a business school. But I was still restless and after finishing that, I decided to come back to Sydney to return to my roots. My only relative is my Aunt Rosa in Sydney."

"What did she think about your coming to New Guinea?"

Julia laughed. "She was in the middle of polishing her

nails when I told her. She objected and was almost in tears. But then the doorbell rang. Her gentleman friend had arrived early, and she forgot to object anymore. Her social calendar is always full, so I doubt she will miss me much."

They climbed in silence for a while, William matching his climb to hers. "William, you seem quite settled here. When I first met you in Sydney, you seemed lonely."

"I was. I do like it here. A man has time to contemplate life here and meet it in a more relaxed manner. The dirt and slums of city life always depress me."

When they reached the spot William had indicated, she found it was an indentation in the side of the mountain, large enough for about ten people to sit inside comfortably. Nearly winded, she turned around and sat down, her breath escaping in a long "Oooooohhh—" at the sight. There was the whole Bulai Valley spread out before her: dark greens and lighter greens, paths crisscrossing in various directions like thin, brown strings wrapped around the hills, with miniature people moving on the road below. The airstrip was a long, white sheet on a mossy bed. The sun was behind them casting shadows of trees in varying lengths that marched down the slope below them. A waterfall was silver filigree against emerald velvet. Such a ruggedly beautiful view hurt her throat. For once she was speechless.

William let her take it all in for a while. "Only 50 years ago there were no white people in this valley—Australian government men had just found it. Bulai people were still in the Stone Age, but they no longer practiced cannibalism. The first wheels they ever saw were the wheels on a government airplane."

"Hadn't they even a potter's wheel? Or a wagon, or cart or anything?"

"No. They knew nothing about a wheel."

"Then how did they travel? How did they transport things?"

"They didn't travel, except by walking every once in a

while. Whatever they transport is still carried on their backs. They didn't travel then because of their fear of everyone else. Living in its own language area, each group was a unit within itself. These mountains hemmed them in, a natural barrier which kept *them* in and the *world* out. They made their own agricultural instruments out of wood and sharpened cassowary bones and bamboo. They grew their own food and made salt out of grasses. Their lives were a continual round of each clan fighting every other clan—battling and head hunting."

"Are you sure there are no cannibals around any more?"

"Not any more."

"How did they make their cooking pots?" Julia asked.

"They didn't cook in pots and still don't. They bury sweet potatoes or yams in hot ashes. There is no set time for them to eat; they just keep their potatoes in hot ashes and eat whenever they are hungry. They make waterpots by simply shaping clay around their hands and baking it in ashes. But many men still carry water in long bamboo poles."

"It's true, then, that their first sight of wheels was when they saw a government airplane?"

"Yes. When the first two government men made a landing on that level place where the airstrip is, people living nearby were scared to death; they all disappeared into the bush. Little by little their curiosity got the upper hand. They thought the airplane was some big bird which the spirits had sent, so later they crept out of the bush bringing yams as a gift to the big spirit bird. Then they got down on their hands and knees and crawled under the plane, looking around to see whether the bird was male or female."

Julia laughed.

"The government men stayed to set up a post. Later, another government plane came in low and dropped supplies for them. Then people were sure that the spirit birds were female because they were dropping eggs!"

"They must have been petrified at the roar of the bird."

"They were. The first government building here was the big house on top of that hill," he said, pointing. "They set up their governing post and began to win the confidence of the people."

"When did the missionaries come?"

"They began to come shortly after. In this country as soon as a government post is established, there are many requests for permission to bring a mission into the area. Since then the missionaries have reduced the Bulai language to writing, set up various schools out over the hills, evangelized the people and established churches. They've built roads, houses and airstrips and brought in all kinds of equipment for bettering the area. They had to fell trees to put in the dam and power plant. Our present missionaries did that. They are a great addition to the area. Papua New Guinea became independent of Australia in 1975. The western section of New Guinea is Indonesian territory." William stopped for breath.

But Julia was full of questions. "What kind of religion did the Bulai people have before?"

"They were, and most still are, animists. They believe that spirits live in every rock and tree. Lightning and thunder are spirits, too. Any dead relative can become a bad spirit and work harm against them."

"Work harm? How do you mean, William?"

He looked quickly at Julia and smiled. "Good girl! That 'William' is coming out just fine."

She made a face at him. "Go on. How do you mean that spirits work harm?"

"Well, if two people fight or have a bad feeling against each other, one may 'put a spell' on the other. Once the other person finds out about it, he dies."

"*Dies?* Just like that?"

"Just like that. From the power of suggestion, no doubt. But it works. I've heard of several cases. They suggest to the intended victim that something has been put inside his or her body which will have a deadly effect. Of course, the victim fully believes this and soon dies, sometimes exactly at the time it has been predicted. Sometimes they call it 'putting the *Dewel*,' or devil, on a person."

Julia shivered and changed the subject. "How long do you suppose you will stay in New Guinea, William? After your next two years are up will you come back for another term?"

"Don't know. I suppose that depends upon when, or if, I find my pearl."

Julia looked blank. "Sorry, you've lost me somewhere."

"Well," William leaned back and contemplated the ever-changing fusion of sunlight and shadow, "I suppose you could say I have an historical hang-up."

She sighed. "I'm still lost."

"Were you good at history in school? Did you ever study Australian history?"

"Some, before we went to America. I suppose I made fairly good grades, but I never heard of a 'historical hang-up.'"

"Does the name 'Moresby' mean anything to you?"

"Uh—I seem to remember a Captain Moresby, and of course there's Port Moresby here in New Guinea. Was it named for him?"

"Yes. Ever heard of the name 'Banner' before?"

She shook her head. "You're the first."

"Uh-huh. I don't mean to embarrass you, but I suppose the fact that you haven't heard of a Banner before is part of my hang-up. Not too many people have. You see, in the 1860s there was a Captain Moresby and a Captain Banner, both captains of sailing ships. Captain Moresby found an island which is now called 'Warrior Island' and discovered pearls there. Somehow he acquired a large gem of a pearl. Just a few years later, Captain Banner also found the island with pearls all over the place. Kids were playing with them like marbles. But before Captain Banner could get any of the pearls for himself, he died. He was an ancestor of mine.

"So ever since, the Banners have been a little jealous of

the Moresbys for having an extremely valuable pearl to hand down from generation to generation. It's a kind of social insurance policy. I'm one of the Banner boys, interested in finding a pearl for myself. Maybe not a pearl, maybe gold. And if I do, maybe my social status will be up to the Moresby's."

"You mean literally find gold? Is that why you became a mining engineer?"

"Yes."

"Well, I hope you find it; it'd be nice to have a rich friend. It probably won't make you a bit nicer, though."

He preened a little. "That's true, of course! It's only my fatal charm that all the girls fall for!"

They both laughed.

Mists were beginning to obscure the mountaintops around them and Julia began shivering.

"You're getting cold," he noticed. "I've been thoughtless. You aren't used to this altitude. Lesson's over for today." He pulled her to her feet, and they made their way back down the hill. By the time they reached the house, a light rain was dancing on the roof of the Land Rover.

"Come in, Julia. You too, William," Mary called from the door. "You haven't had much time to look over the house, so why don't you wander around a bit while I get some tea ready?"

William and Julia walked around looking over the house. It was simply built of wood with wooden floors and the familiar corrugated roof like she'd seen on all the buildings there. A very large water tank stood outside the house, as tall as the house itself and about 12 feet across. A complicated system of gutters from all parts of the house fed into the tank.

"Is that how we get all our water? Just from the skies and off the roof?"

"Yes. We all have these tanks. It rains almost every afternoon here, so we are never desperate for water. If we go three days without rain, everybody thinks we're in a drought. We have a rain gauge at the office, and some of the Bulai people think it is magic. They have the idea that instead of the gauge telling us how much rain has already come, it will *make* the rain come. Sometimes we see someone creeping up very carefully and pouring rain out of the gauge, and guess what? Often the rain stops! They occasionally tell us, "We have enough rain now, so pour it out of your magic glass. If you keep making it come, we can't go hunting."

"I suppose it would take a lifetime to get to know these people and the reason for all their ideas."

"Yes, I suppose it would."

The house was compactly built. A small sitting room was furnished with wicker chairs. The bedrooms had steel folding beds with shelves built into the walls. The shower was connected only to cold water, and Julia couldn't imagine taking a cold shower in this altitude. But connected to pulleys was a bucket punched full of holes. Someone was a genius! Hot water could be put into the bucket for a miniature shower. There was also a tin tub. Julia had a sudden vision of fussy Aunt Rosa taking a bath in such a tub and she couldn't suppress a giggle.

"I just had a mental picture of Aunt Rosa in that tub," she explained to William, "and it struck me as funny. She's just about the most fastidious female you ever saw. You must meet her sometime."

He nodded. "I'd love to."

The kitchen boasted a small wood stove elevated on cement blocks to make it a comfortable height for working on. A hot-water reservoir was built into the side of the stove and a large pile of firewood was stacked behind it. "Do we have to chop all that wood, Mary?" asked Julia.

Mary smiled. "No, we have a man hired for that job. He also keeps the hot-water tank in the stove filled up. Everytime I'm trying to get a small amount of water really hot for a shower, he comes in and pours another bucket of cold water into the reservoir. A lukewarm shower is the best we'll ever get unless we stand guard over the stove all the time."

A small dining area jutted off from the kitchen with a woven mat carpet covering the floor and moss-green cotton drapes hanging at the windows. A folding gate-legged table and steel folding chairs completed the furnishings. A bright flowered cloth covered the table, and it was set with cheerful, yellow plastic dishes. Julia couldn't help but have a pang of nostalgia for Aunt Rosa's Haviland arranged on her Belgian linen cutwork. Candlelight always flickered for Aunt Rosa's dinners.

"How did you get all this furniture here?" Julia asked.

"To bring it by plane is the only way. Not only the furniture, but also every piece of the building material for our house. Each of us waited day by day to get a house, literally piece by piece. The plane came in once a day in good weather. Then we waited day after day to get our furniture the same way." Mary laughed. "One day we got the plastic dishes and a box of pots and pans, but we had no stove. Then the beds came in but it was days before we could get any pillows or covers. When the dining table arrived we had to sit on the floor, for the chairs arrived a month later. Finally I had a home. I will enjoy having you share it with me, Julia." Mary had large, expressive brown eyes. Her movements in the kitchen were light and quick. "Ready for tea?"

Julia suddenly realized how hungry she was. "I'm starved!" she replied. She had eaten very little that day. When she boarded the dawn flight in Port Moresby there had been time for only coffee and toast at the hotel, and she and William had been walking and talking most of the afternoon. She'd completely forgotten about lunch.

William gasped. "My face is red," he apologized. "I had some sandwiches and coffee in the Land Rover. But I must confess I was so excited about being with you that I forgot all about food when we started up the mountain." He touched her hand for a moment. "Please forgive me for being so keyed up that I nearly starved you to death. I'll go get the sandwiches." He dashed out to the Land Rover and came in with a plastic-wrapped packet, rain glistening on his hair.

Mary had prepared some deviled eggs and hot muffins. The muffins were delicious with Australian butter and jam. William's tinned beef sandwiches rounded out the meal. Nothing had tasted so good to Julia in a long time. "I hope I'm not this hungry every day. I could put on 10 pounds a day with teas like this!"

"The altitude always makes one hungry at first," William explained, "then our appetites begin to settle down to normal. Julia, I hope you'll come to my house and have dinner with me in a few days. I have a servant named Sekiba who is a real jewel. He loves to show off his cooking. He was trained in a hotel in Port Moresby."

"Thank you, I'll look forward to it." With the warm tea inside her, she could barely keep her eyes open and yawned widely. "Oh, excuse me, it isn't the company, it's just—"

"The altitude," chorused Mary and William. "It's the way it affects some people at first. But others come up here and can't sleep a wink the first night they are here."

"So I'll go and let you sleep," William excused himself. He held her hand for a moment. "I'm so very glad you are here, Julia, and I hope you will be happy. In fact I'm going to see to it that you are." He smiled. "'Bye, see you soon."

"Good night, William, I'm glad you are here too. Thank you for a happy arrival. I know I will love it here."

After William left, Mary helped her unpack, hang up her dresses and arrange things on the shelves in the wall. The shelves were covered with a cotton print curtain strung on wire across the top. The curtain was of the same material as the bedspread. Mary hadn't had much to work with, but she showed a flair for making an otherwise drab place homey and inviting. Julia was grateful for her warm splashes of color but determined to order other things from Australia which would make their house more comfortable. She was too sleepy at that moment, however, even to decide what those things might be.

She undressed and slid between cold sheets on the narrow, steel bed. Her toes curled up seeking a warm spot and couldn't find one. Just then Mary came in carrying a hot-water bottle which she had wrapped with a flannel cloth. This she put under the covers at Julia's feet, and Julia's toes wiggled for sheer joy.

Her feet didn't itch a bit.

"Oh, Mary, that's heavenly!" She was asleep before Mary could leave and close the door.

Chapter 4

*T*he next day Julia walked with Mary from their house to the engineering office to report for her first day of work. The office was drab in comparison to most offices she'd seen. It was furnished with steel tables for desks, steel folding chairs and files. On the tables were two manual typewriters and woven mats covered the floor. Grant's desk was in one corner of the room.

Mary showed her the filing system, which didn't seem very complicated. On her desk a stack of handwritten letters was ready for her to decipher and type, and Mary laughed when Julia groaned over their boss's handwriting. "You'll get used to that. Once you can read his writing, you'll see he is precise in expressing his thoughts. You won't have to worry about editing his letters, and he's nice to work for."

Julia settled down to work, but her eyes kept straying out the window. The glass framed majestic mountain peaks with long, green *kunai* grass marching to the top. It waved in the wind—no that wasn't right, it *billowed* in the wind. Thin, brown shoestring paths laced their way up through the rippling green. She found it difficult to work and ignore such grandeur.

The days flew by and she began to feel at home. Over Grant's desk came correspondence concerning every phase of life of the Bulai people. Julia soon became aware of many problems, ranging from a man's inhumane treatment of his wives, to settling a quarrel over wages and the prevention of clashes between clans that had been enemies for centuries. They came to Grant's attention because when disagreements arose between people who were supposed to work together, the work stopped. Many times the persons involved didn't seem in any hurry to bring peace.

Julia enjoyed working with Grant and Mary and had to learn a whole new vocabulary of New Guinea terms, some amusing, some tragic. She learned, for example, that people in the Bulai area said they got angry in their intestines and they loved in their lungs. Memory and fear were located in the ear and pleasure in the stomach. "I'm putting my stomach for you," meant, "I am pleased with you." One did not smell an odor, one *heard* an odor. To "pull one's ear" didn't mean literally. It meant talking to someone, trying to get him to do something he shouldn't do, to tempt him.

One day she learned something about the dread *Kuru* disease or "laughing disease," which used to afflict only women.

"Why did it afflict only women?" Julia inquired.

"Kuru disease is similar in manifestations to Parkinson's disease. But in the past when people were cannibals, only women were given human brains—their portion from every enemy killed. Eating human brains caused a long, slow death. Scientists came to this conclusion after studying the disease for a long time. Men and boys ate other portions of human flesh. They believed in *mana*."

Julia shuddered. "Mana? What's that?"

"It's the belief that everything has a kind of mystical power. So the person eating that thing would take on or assimilate the mana. If anyone ate parts of the chief of a tribe, for example, the chief's mana would enter the other person and make him strong. Back in their history their lives were a continual round of cannibalistic fighting. Thank God, those days are over!"

"After hearing all that, I'd leave for Australia this afternoon if we had an afternoon plane!" Julia shuddered again. "Sure those days are over?"

Mr. Richards nodded.

Julia began to realize that some governmental laws, as well as missionary work, struck at the very heart of the ancient civilization of Papua New Guinea. For centuries any man had been able to beat any of his wives for such a misdemeanor as failing to raise a good crop of sweet potatoes. A law forbidding wife-beating, instituted after Australia began to govern, therefore, was not widely appreciated. Money wages had been introduced into a society used to trading in pearl shells and pigs. So there was bound to be tension among people who had money to pay for wives and those who still had to trade pigs for them. A law had been passed making it compulsory to bury a dead body. Formerly, a body had simply been left in a tree, or among some of the tribes, smoked and put into a house or cave.

"Mary, it's hard to take in some of these facts." Julia and Mary were sitting near the kitchen stove and reading after supper. "Some of these customs are absolutely unbelievable! I was reading about how they used to smoke a body."

"I know it's nearly unbelievable. But the people of this country have come a long way in just 50 years, Julia. It hasn't been easy for them to jump from the Stone Age into the Space Age. In our country, we've had many years to develop our ideas and civilization. These people have had little time. It's surprising they have adjusted as quickly as they have."

"Do you think they understand that laws are made to try and help them?"

"I'm sure they do not understand at all why some of their customs can no longer be tolerated. Of course, they would develop even faster, but one of the major problems of this land is the unbelievable number of languages."

"How many different languages are there?"

"I've heard about 520, but I don't suppose anyone knows for sure. Most of the men in government can speak pidgin, and it's spoken on the coast. But certainly not all new Guineans do. Sometimes only a few hundred people will speak one language, sometimes a few thousand. Then just over the mountain ridge will be a different tribe of people with an entirely different language. In the last few years many, many schools have been established. Lots of people are learning English as well as pidgin. It's a big job to teach everybody English, but someday it may happen."

Julia got up to put some water on the stove. "Want some tea?"

"Yes, that sounds good."

Julia asked, "How does missionary work help to change some of these customs? Missionaries must have a very hard time living here."

"They do," Mary answered. "But it makes a tremendous difference in people's lives. And it takes years. Missionaries must first win their confidence before New Guinea people will accept anything they says. But when missionaries prove they are friends, then the people begin to listen."

"What changes when a New Guinea man becomes a Christian?"

"It's not easy for him to desert tribal customs, but some practices he *must* refuse to follow. And when a man puts his faith in God, he can overcome a lot of his fears."

"What are his biggest fears?" Julia peeked to see whether the water was boiling.

Mary thought for a moment. "I suppose his biggest fears are of evil spirits, witch doctors and those who might 'put the Dewel' on him."

"What about his habits? Do they soon change?"

"Well, some changes are soon apparent. Christian people stop stealing each other's pigs and wives—and they are important in that order—and they stop fighting. Their houses are cleaner and neater. Then too, Christian men don't beat their wives or marry more than one wife. Neither do they insist on tattooing their children."

"What about that awful habit of chopping off fingers or pieces of ears to show they are mourning when someone in the family dies?" Julia asked.

"You are right, Julia. That is an awful habit. I've heard missionaries say that when they first came here, the New Guinea people used to look at their white hands and could see that none of the fingers were missing. So they would ask the missionaries, 'Don't you love your people? When they die, why don't you show you love them? We do! See how many fingers we've cut off?'

"It's a terrible thing because sometimes when they cut off a finger or part of an ear, that place becomes infected and sometimes they die. But Christians don't do that anymore."

"I've seen people with only one finger left on a hand!" Julia exclaimed.

"Yes. And many Christians are lacking fingers because their parents chopped off joints when they were children and before they heard anything about being a Christian. Of course, the missions set up schools too, and with education some of their old superstitions fade away."

Julia put a pinch of black tea in a pot and poured in boiling water. While it steeped she went to her room and brought back a treat, a new tin of chocolate cookies—"biscuits" to the Australians. "Surprise!"

"Oh!" Mary was pleased. "What a *nice* surprise!"

As they drank their tea and munched the biscuits, Julia pursued the conversation. "I've often heard people in America say, 'Let the happy little native alone—don't thrust civilization upon him!' What do you think about that?"

Mary shook her head. "People who say that haven't been around here! Nowhere that I know of in Papua New Guinea have the 'happy little natives' been free from war or the power of evil spirits. They all fear sorcery, disease and hunger due to crop failure. Missions and government are both helping them to better their lives. Our company helps, too, but plenty of problems still exist."

Julia learned about one problem which flared up sporadically, depending upon how active the leaders were. This was the "Cargo Cult." People belonging to this cult believed that their great ancestors, who were now good spirits, had made things such as airplanes, axes, knives, shovels and, most of all, pearl shells. Their ancestors had sent the goods back to the new Guinea people, but white people had hijacked the cargo and now they made the natives work for these things. This cult arose in various places and with new vigor and innovations from time to time. Some natives had built jetties and houses for the reception of great cargo which, they felt, would be coming from their ancestors by boat. Others had been known to slash down their banana plantations because they believed by some miracle that something much better than bananas would mysteriously appear. Of course, along with this belief was native jealousy of white and educated people for having so many "things." Sometimes this gave rise to violent clashes.

The patient explanation, by those who knew better, of the fact that white people *and* colored people worked and *made* all these things in another country, was hard for the New Guinean to understand. He did not *see* the things made. Nor did he see the white men in New Guinea actually *pay* for the goods they had. They were usually paid for by a check, not with shells and/or pigs. This could not be understood by a primitive-economy man. Many were certain that white men had robbed them of their own imagined cargo. At times dangerous confrontations erupted over this. The people of this cult had been pathetically misled by some leaders with delusions of grandeur.

When Western manufactured goods appeared in New Guinea, another subtle problem developed. This was the loss of a native's pride in his own creations. Granted that some of the handmade things were artistic—such as carved, wooden pieces, handwoven bark belts, bamboo flutes and combs, necklets of pigs' teeth and *tapa* (bark) cloth. But these articles could not compare with the glamorous appearance or utility of machine-made articles imported from Australia. So when a native saw manufactured articles—bright beads, cotton goods and strong tools—he was bound to feel that what he could make was inferior and insignificant. Tools from civilization designed to help the native do his subsistence work better, such as steel axes, spades, knives, gave him more time to create things with his hands. But the irony was he often felt his handmade items were no longer worth making. Everyone wanted something foreign. It is always a great loss when a nation loses pride in its own culture.

William stuck his head in the door one day just before noon. "Hi, Julia. Getting on to our system of doing things?"

"The system is easy. It's the superstition around here that gets me sometimes!"

"I told you," he teased, "no sissies invited!"

"If I had been a sissy, I'd have gone home before now," she declared. "Have you been busy? I haven't seen you lately."

He came in and sat by her desk. "Yes, I've been out on a tour in the district, but I was anxious to get back to see how you were."

"What do you do when you're on tour?"

"Well, our workers are looking for possible oil well sites. And of course, as I told you, I'd like to find gold in some of these digging places. So I go out and check on them to see how things are going. I bring back soil samples and run tests." He smiled at her. "I have to go out again for a few days, but when I come back I hope you will come over for dinner. Sekiba is already excited about cooking dinner for a lady."

It was Julia's turn to tease. "Haven't you ever had a lady over for dinner before? There are other single girls here in Bulai."

"Never wanted to show off my etchings before. I only show my etchings to redheads," he said with a grin. "Now that you've come, I can't wait to show them to you. And, of course, this will give Sekiba something to think about."

"He has you to think about."

"Yes, but he's been moody lately. One of his good friends died, as a result of 'putting the Dewel' he says, so he's been very sad."

"Was it a case of black magic?"

"It must have been. Tiba was young, Sekiba's age, and nothing seemed wrong with him before. Sekiba says Tiba's uncle did it. "Well," he touched her shoulder, "I have to go now. Work hard and miss me a little."

Julia smiled at him. "That won't be too hard."

Even though Grant and Mary were busy at their desks, the office seemed empty after William left.

The days that followed were filled with work at the office, and after work Julia washed her clothes by hand, wrote letters to Aunt Rosa and to Dave Hanson in Kentucky and tried to get used to cooking on the wood stove. Mary was far ahead of her concerning the latter.

Of course some of it was more or less drudgery, but there was a constant feeling of excitement about living in New Guinea. She awoke in the mornings with an air of expectancy, knowing she would learn something that day and feel something never experienced before. She wanted to get well acquainted with the Bulai people and their culture.

People were constantly wandering in and out of the office—some clothed, some wearing only bark belts with netting (*billum* drape) in front and green *tangket* leaves in the back. They came to see Mr. Richards about a great variety of problems. Julia began to understand some words in pidgin and in the Bulai language. Her ears were tuned keenly because she realized that, in order to understand the people, she would have to learn something of their language. Common sense told her it would take many years to learn any New Guinea language and she had signed up for only two. Nevertheless, she was elated and determined that, as long as she was in New Guinea, she would study. She would strain to overcome language barriers and to also learn the unspoken clues of behavior. Both were necessary to understand the Bulai culture. The newspaper advertisement in the Sydney paper had been right. It was indeed a challenge.

William came into the office five days later. "Hi! I hope you missed me."

"You're conceited enough already. I refuse to admit that I did."

"Please admit it," he pleaded with a smile. "All yesterday slogging through that kunai grass and all the way over the last two ridges, I was saying to myself, 'She's missing me. Oh, how she's missing me!' You have no idea how effective it was to cause me to hurry."

"You're an idiot, William Banner. Did you find any gold or any pearls?"

"No gold. And I think the pearl stayed here."

"You're not an idiot; you're dangerous!"

"How about dinner at my house tonight, Julia? Please come."

"I can't think of anything I'd rather do."

"I'll come for you about seven o'clock, all right?"

"Right," she smiled.

Julia was excited. It had been a long time since she'd met a man with such a zest for living. He was extremely intelligent and fun to be with, but she suspected he had a deep side to his nature, not yet discovered. She knew he liked her a great deal and she responded to that. She admitted to herself that it had been mostly his enthusiasm about New Guinea which had sold her on the idea of coming in the first place. The thought struck her, *Wouldn't this be a drab place with no William?* Then instantly, *Thank goodness that is only a thought and not a reality!*

After work she washed and rinsed her hair under the bucket shower, rolled it on curlers and sat beside the kitchen stove to let it dry. She had not known there would be electricity; otherwise she would have brought her portable hair dryer and stereo set. She had already asked Aunt Rosa to send them. Now it was simply a matter of waiting their turn as cargo in the one plane a day.

Julia wore a plaid suit with touches of yellow and orange in the weave to complement the color of her hair. She wanted to look especially nice, but nothing could be done about the visible freckles on her nose except to dust them with powder. They had always kept her more or less humble about believing she was beautiful.

William came in, scrubbed and clean, with a tangy scent of mannish cologne. He looked appreciatively at Julia and held both of her hands. "You're beautiful, Julia!" He was serious. "Your hair is like burnished red-gold. Sometimes I'd like to call you Red. And sometimes I may call you Julie, if it's okay?"

"Sure, if you want to."

William's house was built exactly like hers, but it showed a definite masculine touch with brown and orange pillows on the wicker chairs and a brown and tan braided rug on the floor. A stereo was playing softly, and she noticed the album titles ranged from Bach and Tchaikovsky to baroque guitar, Romeo and Juliet, Van Cliburn and Floyd Cramer's piano— and some light classics. Exactly the kind of music she enjoyed. Definitely not America's hard rock or soul, but not too far on the other side of the generation gap either. Arranged on one wall was a collection of spears and arrows, bright with woven cane and feather decorations.

A tantalizing, spicy odor of baked chicken and dressing pervaded the house. She hadn't smelled that since she'd left Aunt Rosa's. Meat in Bulai was scarce, all of it had to be flown in, and usually canned. They were able to get some vegetables locally—beans, peas, cabbage, pumpkin—and of course the ever-present sweet potatoes, *kau kau*. Everything else was flown in from Australia, so the price of food was extremely high.

"I smell chicken!" Julia inhaled a great breath. "What a

wonderful aroma! Where did you get it, William?"

"Sekiba managed it. If you'd been a passenger on yester-day's plane, you'd have shared a seat with a basket of chick-ens. As I told you, Sekiba learned to cook in a hotel and some of his friends there in Port Moresby sent up the chickens to him. He says he knows what pink-misis like. 'Pink-misis' means white, foreign ladies."

Sekiba came in, bowed slightly and placed a small tray on the table between two wicker chairs. There were crackers and two glasses of tangy tomato juice, spiced with lemon and a little sugar. He smiled widely, showing strong, brilliantly white teeth. Julia judged him to be about 20 years old. He was dressed in a long white skirt and shirt. The skirt was tied at the waist, she knew it was called a *lap-lap*. His clothes were spotlessly clean.

"He certainly is a nice-looking young man, William."

"I told you. He's a real jewel."

"How did you happen to get him?"

"Well, a few years ago when I first arrived in Port Moresby, I was eating dinner in the Darawa Hotel, and this boy came up quietly and stood beside me. He said, 'You laik servant boy, Mastah? Me laik pinim moah bettah wok.' I asked him, 'Will I need a servant boy in this country?' I couldn't understand too much of his pidgin at that time.

"But Sekiba pleaded, 'Supos you go 'long hilands, moah betta me go onetime 'long you.'

"And when I asked him what kind of work he could do, he said, 'Me got savee gud pella tru long washim na ironim cloths, cookim kau kau, no workim strong long garden ogeda sumting. An, Mastah, me savee pulum su su bilong bulla ma cow.' He waved his hands to show me he also knew how to milk a cow."

By that time Julia was laughing at that conglomeration of pidgin.

William grinned too. "Then I asked him how much wages he wanted and he thought a few minutes and came out with,

'Me laik kissim 10 dollas 'long one week, Mastah.'

"I wanted to know why he wished to leave Port Moresby and he grinned. It was too hot there and he was simply homesick for the mountains. I thought it over and the next day told him he could work for me. At that time I was stationed at Port Moresby, but I took him with me on my treks into the hills and that seemed to satisfy him. When I was transferred up here, he was wild with joy. His salary is the best money I've ever spent."

Julia sipped the cold tomato juice. "Mary and I could do with a Sekiba in our kitchen!"

William nodded. "Yes, it would be good for you and Mary to have a native helper, but a girl would be better for you. Maybe we could find a bright girl who would like to work, one that isn't already married with a baby. They marry so young! You could learn a lot about their culture by having someone in your house all the time. And you could also be a help to her, teaching her English and our ways and customs."

"I really do want to learn something of the language and Bulai culture, William. I haven't been here long, but it's beginning to have a fascinating hold on me." She giggled. "My feet haven't itched a bit in the last few weeks!"

"I've disconnected that mysterious radar, Julie. I want you to stay."

She smiled at him. "Have you really learned a lot from Sekiba?"

"Oh, Sekiba is invaluable to me, much more than a servant. He is really a buffer between civilizations and an interpreter of customs. I began to realize that Sekiba's people belong, not to a simple way of life, but to a complex system of ideas, beliefs, practices, traditions and customs. And their way must be handled with care by all of us foreigners who live here."

William stretched out his legs, leaned back and munched some crackers in perfect relaxation as he went on about his native helper. "I was amazed at one thing though. Sekiba outwardly seems sophisticated and has adopted many Australian ways, but he still retains many fears of evil spirits from his childhood. And he is moody—the temperature emanating from our kitchen goes up and down with his moods."

"Is he often in a bad mood?" Julia asked.

"Oh, no. Depending on the circumstances, he's high and low. I think I mentioned to you before I left the other day about his friend dying, and he's been moody ever since that. But last night when I came in, his spirits were lifted."

"What lifted them?"

"Well, this is the whole story. One day Sekiba and the temperature were both down. At dinner he asked, 'Mastah, you savee Tiba? 'Im dai—pinish!'

"Tiba was a Bulai boy, a government employee who was planting trees. He and Sekiba had become good friends. I was shocked. Tiba *dead*? I had seen him only a few days before that, so I asked Sekiba what happened. Sekiba explained it this way: 'Yes, Mastah, Tiba dai. Tiba pite long talk talk his smalpappa,' which means he had a big fight with his uncle. Then Tiba told Sekiba that his uncle had 'put the Dewel' on him and that he would die in two days. So Tiba had died two days later."

"You mean Tiba died just because his uncle *said* so?"

William sipped some juice. "I asked Sekiba the same thing. He said, 'No, Mastah. Tiba dai because smalpappa put Dewel. But smalpappa mo bettah look out 'long. Bepore Tiba dai, 'im say, Dewel come along smalpappa.' So it seems that in retaliation Tiba also put a devil on his uncle. After Tiba died, Sekiba was mumbling hopefully to himself all the time, 'Dewel gonna git 'im smalpappa!' and the kitchen temperature had dropped to a low point when I went on tour a few days ago.

"But this morning I discovered that, two days after I left, Tiba's uncle, who had been quite well, died suddenly while building a house. So Sekiba is satisfied. He reported to me this morning, 'Smalpappa 'im put Dewel on Tiba. Now

Dewel get 'im smalpappa.' He feels justice has been accomplished. So the temperature in the kitchen has been up all day. These Bulai people feel that justice must absolutely be done.

"Now that we're happy around here again, Sekiba has outdone himself on the dinner tonight."

Julia was mystified. "I really don't know what to make of all this talk of evil spirits which exist everywhere for the Bulai people. Of course I have never faced it before. Yet they would never even try to think of any other reason for those deaths, would they? I suppose the spirits *are* everywhere for the Bulais? And no other explanation will *ever* satisfy them for odd things happening?"

"That's right," William answered. "They live in dread all the time because evil spirits cause everything. Even if a Bulai stubs his toes against a stone, *he* didn't do it. The stone kicked him."

William smiled at her. "Let's forget evil spirits, Julie. I have to confess something to you. Sekiba has taken good care of me here, and my life for the past few years has been filled with work and music and fascination with New Guinea. I have always liked the quiet life here. But that day at the airport when you looked at me, smiled and said, 'How do you do, Mr. Terror,' I realized I'd been missing something very important in my life. Maybe I've found it!" He stood up. "Let's go to dinner." He pulled Julia to her feet and led her to the dining room.

Chapter 5

"*M*ary, do you suppose we could bake a chocolate cake in this monstrosity of a stove? I'm hungry for cake, and I have cocoa." Julia and Mary were sitting in the kitchen, folding chairs pulled close to the stove and their feet propped up on another chair. It was Saturday and they were enjoying a late breakfast in the only warm place in the house. Julia had been so busy getting acquainted with the office detail, Bulai beliefs and William that she and Mary had had very little time together to relax.

"Well, I haven't done it yet, but we can try. Is William coming to dinner? If he is, I'll ask Marvin."

Julia had met Marvin but hadn't had a chance to get acquainted with him. "Good. I've already asked William. Tell me about you and Marvin. And will you please make the fire right for the cake? I don't seem to do too well with this stove."

"Well," Mary's face was flushed, "I've known Marvin for six months now and he's a wonderful person." She opened the oven door and put her hand inside to test the heat of it. "I think he loves me, but my salary is larger than his and that bothers him."

"Why?"

"Oh, I don't know, poor but proud, I suppose. He grew up on a sheep ranch in Australia's bush country. It was a small ranch and quite primitive. Living was hard. Marvin didn't want to tend sheep all his life and being mechanically minded, he went to Sydney and learned automobile mechanics. He keeps most of the machinery at the mission station running. He knows tractors, jeeps, Land Rovers, radios, refrigerators—anything with wheels or motors. He even works on our company's and the government's vehicles in his spare time."

"How did Marvin happen to come to New Guinea as a missionary?"

"You see, he has always been a devout person. While he was in Sydney, he joined a prayer group. They were praying especially for missionaries in New Guinea, and when he heard they needed mechanics here, he volunteered. Of course, the mission salary is small."

Julia stretched before the warm stove. "How about you, Mary? Was your life so different in Australia?"

"Oh, yes, I'm a city girl and I've always had an easy life. Since coming here, in response to a challenge in a newspaper advertisement—"

"Oh, so an ad hooked you, too, huh?"

"Yes, it did. I've had to learn to live in a completely new way. It wasn't easy at first to live in a grass house with no heat or hot water or any of the other conveniences I was used to. Then to wait for this house to be built piece by piece wasn't easy either. But I love it here now. The inconveniences never did bother Marvin, but he has the idea that I wouldn't be happy if I had to live here permanently—and he intends to make this his life. He knows he will never be rich, so he keeps a lid on his feelings.

"But I do enjoy working with these New Guinea people. They are simple but responsive, and their old ways are changing."

"Are you religious too, Mary? How would that side of your life fit in with Marvin's?"

Mary put some more wood into the stove. "I didn't use to be religious at all. I didn't even believe in God and never went to church. But Marvin has taught me a lot about being a Christian. Marvin is such a genuine person, kind and considerate and self-giving to everybody. And he has a great faith in God. His faith isn't at all complicated; he just believes the Bible and lives by it every day. Let me tell you what happened just a short while before you came."

Mary poured each of them a second cup of coffee. "Marvin and I were taking a load of supplies out to a New Guinea pastor who lives in a small village. When we got there a crowd of people met us in the yard. They were all excited. The minister told Marvin that one of his parishioners, a woman named Manee, was inside and very sick. We asked what was wrong with her. The minister said, 'She will probably die because another woman put the devil on her. The other woman thinks that Manee is trying to get her husband, so she told Manee that the devil would come and get her in three days. This is the third day. Manee ran here this morning and is now inside our house, scared to death and just waiting for the devil. She says she can only wait to die, that's all. She won't listen to me—won't let me pray with her.'

"Marvin asked the minister, 'Did you say she's a Christian and a member of your village church?' The pastor said, 'Yes, will you please go in and talk to her?'

"Marvin asked me to come in too. I must admit I was frightened, but I went inside the small *pit-pit* house with Marvin and the pastor."

"What is a pit-pit house?" Julia interrupted. "I've heard the term but nobody has explained it to me."

"It's what all the Bulai houses are made of, that tall, coarse kunai grass growing everywhere. They weave the grass flat on the ground in lengths big enough for one side of the house."

"Oh, I'd just been calling them 'grass houses,'" Julia replied.

Mary continued, "Well, we went into that pastor's house and the woman on the low bed looked terrified. Her eyes were rolling. Marvin touched her forehead and said gently, 'Manee, are you a Christian?' and the woman nodded. Her eyes looked wild. Then Marvin said, 'Don't you believe that God is stronger than the devil?' She hesitated, looked around as if too frightened to answer and then nodded again. Marvin kept his hand on her forehead, closed his eyes and prayed. He talked to God so simply and asked him not to let the devil come near Manee at all. He asked God to stop the devil way out in the jungle. Such a simple prayer like that, but it meant so much to the woman! She began to calm down a little. Then Marvin said, 'Manee, I command the devil in Jesus' name not to come near you at all. Not ever! Your life is not over, for God has work for you to do.'

"Then Marvin spoke to her in a strong, commanding voice and said, 'Now, Manee, get up out of that bed and go back home and pay attention only to your own husband! Pray and work and behave yourself! Then the devil can never harm you!'

"And you know, Julia, Manee got right up off that bed, walked past us and all those in the yard, went to her home, got her cassowary-bone hoe and started digging sweet potatoes for her family's supper! She hasn't been sick a day since."

Julia gasped. "What a story! Almost like those in the Bible about Jesus casting out demons! Had Manee been trying to get the other woman's husband?"

Mary nodded. "We heard she had. But she was so scared that day, I don't believe she will ever try it again."

"What about the woman who had put the curse on Manee?"

"You know, the strange thing was that her curse boomeranged, as the New Guinea people say it does sometimes. About two weeks later, while standing under a tree during a storm, that woman was struck by lightning and died. Now the people in that village always ask Marvin to pray for them for one thing or another.

"I was proud of Marvin that day. He knew just what to do. I was scared to be in such a situation, but Marvin said, 'Why, Mary, you just have to pray and have faith. God doesn't want the devil to get any of his children. And even though Manee had been converted and baptized, it was hard for her to let go of her fear of the bad spirits.'

"That did a lot for my faith, Julia. Knowing Marvin is making me examine my own beliefs, or lack of belief, more than I ever did before. With his help, I might even be able to lead a prayer meeting sometime." She laughed and added two more sticks of wood to the stove. "Are you religious, Julia?"

"Well—yes," Julia hedged. "I believe in God and not just fate. I've always gone to Sunday school, and I taught a Sunday school class of girls in America. I've never thought too much about being religious. I do read the Bible sometimes though."

"I didn't think much about it when I first met Marvin. But he says that I must decide where I stand. I guess everybody will have to decide where to stand. Do you believe that?"

Julia thought for a while. "Yes, I suppose that's true. I've heard some ministers say they believe God has a plan for every life and that we ought to discover it. Ever heard of that?"

Mary sipped her coffee. "No, not just like that, but I hope that God intends for Marvin and me somehow to fit into that plan together. I'm truly in love with him. Sometimes I wonder whether I should let him know how much I love him or whether that would only scare him off. He has to know sometime!"

Mary jumped up. "The fire is burning well and we can start your cake." She got out a large mixing bowl and a hand beater. "Marvin teases me about learning to cook on this wood stove, but I've learned lots of things. I even had to learn how to bake bread. There isn't any bread here at all, so it's mine or none."

"It's very good bread you've been making. You must

teach me how. Does Marvin like it?"

"I guess so. I suppose he was getting desperate for some bread because one day he made a bargain with me. He said, 'I'll be glad to eat your burned bread anytime, lady, if you'll just allow my muddy shoes to come into your neat little kitchen. And while I'm here, I'll repair any broken motors you have lying around.'"

Julia and Mary alternately laughed and despaired as the cake progressed. First the stove got too hot and they were afraid to put the cake in. When it cooled down a bit they slid the pan gently inside. Then it got too cool. Finally, they stood for an hour and hand-fed the fire just one stick of wood at a time. The cake was lopsided, but it did rise.

Making icing was a problem too, because the sugar was large-grained and gray-looking. Julia didn't see how raw sugar would ever melt in any three-minute icing. So they made a boiled icing and put pink coloring in it to combat the battle-gray. Then they slit the cake through the middle, making two layers, and turned it lop-side to good-side. By that time they'd laughed so hard they were practically in hysterics.

Marvin and William came in for dinner, scrubbed, shaved and handsome. Odd how just two men in a room filled up the whole place! Marvin looked tenderly at Mary, a look which Julia caught, but Mary had just turned to bring in the cake. Julia glanced at William and met a gaze so intent that she blushed and looked away. William's presence was becoming more and more important to her.

Marvin was lavish with praise for the cake. "It's just wonderful," he grinned with his mouth full, "especially with no other cake available in Bulai."

William nodded solemnly and made a great show of washing it down with a cup of tea.

The weeks flew by punctuated by letters from Aunt Rosa, clucking over Julia's well-being and with social news of Sydney. "Are you sure you are getting good food? How can you stand weather that rains every day with no fireplace in your bedroom? You speak only of William Banner in your letters; aren't there any *other* eligible men in New Guinea? I've looked the Banners up in the social register. They come from a good family line, but they are so *poor*—

"I met a wonderful man at a dinner the other evening. He's too young for me but just right for you. When you have your leave, I'll have a dinner party and invite him. He has everything: wealth, social position, looks, breeding. You'd be a beautiful pair.

"Frederick is still calling. He wants to marry me, but I think I prefer the arrangement as it is. It's more exciting this way, and I don't have to get up for breakfast! The styles this year are more feminine than ever. My spring suit is . . . ."

Aunt Rosa would never change!

It was hard for Julia to believe she'd been away from Sydney nearly seven months. Where had the time gone?

William came by the office one Friday afternoon. "Hi, Julie. Miss me, I hope?"

"Well, William Banner! You've been gone a long, long time."

"Right. I haven't seen you for four weeks, seven hours and five minutes to be exact."

"Really? I'm surprised you had it counted up so correctly." She didn't tell him it had seemed much longer.

His eyes crinkled at the corners. "You mean you counted, too?"

Julia blushed. "Yes, I did miss you. Where have you been so long?"

"I was out over the highlands in a place which, to get there, took a week of trekking, a week to get back, and I stayed there two weeks testing soil samples."

"You didn't go alone, did you?"

"Oh, no, I never do. I went with several others in our company from Port Moresby, plus some carriers and cooks. Sekiba was along."

"Well, welcome back to Bulai!"

"Let's have a picnic tomorrow. Please say you will."

"All right, where shall we go?"

"We'll find a beautiful spot and relax. Wear some strong walking shoes."

The next day they drove out in William's Land Rover about 10 miles from home base. Then he parked the Rover and they climbed, following a narrow path as it wound through a deep forest and angled up around a mountain. William walked in front, continually stopping and turning to help her over a narrow or dangerous place. They had to stoop low to encircle a jutting rock; then suddenly, there in front of them was a sparkling waterfall. It fell down from a towering ridge to their right, splashing over a long ledge of rock into a natural basin below. Large stones in the basin sent a spray out in all directions, and sunlight filtering through the green canopy of the forest created a rainbow of color across the spray.

"Oh, what a beautiful spot! How did you ever find it?"

"I didn't really. An old chief showed it to me. Said it belonged to his family. He's a friend of mine, and after we eat, I'll take you to meet him. He will be pleased that we came to see him. We can sit on this ledge. Does it make you too dizzy to sit up here?"

"Not if I don't look down."

William took his knapsack and water bottle off his shoulders. They ate lunch with their backs against the mountain and their legs stretched out in front of them on the narrow ledge. Breathtaking views of rugged New Guinea spread out in a semi-circle before them.

They ate leisurely, discussing everything from Middle East problems, to drugs, computers, the arts and Nicaragua. William was stimulating in discussion, and he seemed to appreciate Julia's ideas. Slowly their conversation wound down until they relaxed in comfortable silence. Julia's hand was resting lightly in William's.

Julia took a deep breath. "Just sitting here and looking at all this wild grandeur awes me. New Guinea seems like such a magnificent waste. Most of the world will never be able to appreciate it. God must have been pleased when he finished such beauty as this. Do you believe in God, William?"

"Of course I believe in God. But before I came to New Guinea, I hadn't much time to think about him. My life was too rushed. But here a man has time to contemplate and weigh situations and people."

"I remember you said in Sydney that you were depressed."

"I was. But since coming here, I've seen how belief in God can change a native from a person who is afraid of all kinds of evil spirits to one not at all fearful. I've seen cruel men become kind. When I look at the missionaries and see their work and know how little they are paid for what they do, I am continually amazed at their dedication to God. They are either grossly misguided or what they believe is true and their dedication is complete. I've had some conversations with Marvin about this." He finished his sandwich and took a drink of water.

"So," Julia asked, "you have come to the conclusion that missionaries are not misguided?"

He gazed across the deep valley below to another mountain peak rising opposite them. "Right. Sometimes I think they are the only ones who are *not* misguided."

Julia leaned her head back against the towering rock wall behind them. "Why do you say that?"

He held her hand in both of his. "Well, Julie, this last month I've had a lot of time to think. One day while testing soil samples, with the hope of finding gold, the thought suddenly struck me that my motive was all wrong. My reason for working here and trying to find gold for myself, just so I could match up to the Moresby boys, was a flimsy reason for living. It just didn't cut it! Somehow, once I realized that, other things fell into place. Now the goal of getting rich and well-known in Sydney society is gone. And I feel relieved over it. I think knowing you had something to do with it."

"How could it? We haven't talked about this before."

"No." He looked earnestly at her. "Julie, I am almost certain I'm in love with you. I don't think you feel the same way, but maybe someday you will. I guess I've decided that I want what's really important in life—your love. Maybe someday God will give you to me."

She looked down at their hands, and tears stung her eyes. William hadn't asked for a thing, just simply stated his feelings. She said slowly, "I . . . I don't know what to say—"

He leaned close and kissed her lightly.

"Hey!" she exclaimed. "This is a dangerous place to start kissing. I'd have a long way to fall for you!"

He grinned and his seriousness vanished. "We have lots of time. Just stick around, Julie. That's enough for me now. Come on, let's go see a chief who used to be cruel and now is kind." He pulled her to her feet and guided her back down to the green-covered trail. They soon came out into a small clearing. In the middle of the open space was a giant tree, which William pointed out to her as the village *sing-sing* tree.

"What does that mean?"

"This is the sacred tree around and under which the villagers have their special dances and feasts. This tree is the center of all village activity."

All about this opening in the forest were scattered pit-pit houses. The pit-pit was woven in symmetrical designs along the house walls, and the roofs were thatched and very low.

An old man saw them coming and emerged from his hut to meet them. The chief! He wore only the usual bark belt, which bit into his side, with the billum drape in front and green leaves behind. His body and face bore deep scars of battle, and he had other blue marks which were tattoos within scars. White feathers decorated his head. He smiled a greeting with betel-nut red teeth and seemed genuinely glad to see William.

A shorter old man came out of the small door of a different house. He was dressed like the chief but had thick, parallel tattooed lines marching down his face. He wore red feathers in his wooly hair. They motioned for William and Julia to sit down, which they did in the shade of the huge tree in the middle of the clearing. The first old man called a woman from his house and gave an order. She soon brought out a handful of sweet potatoes and gave them to Julia, saying something Julia couldn't understand. Then she smiled, and her teeth were also red.

Julia nodded and smiled her thanks. Some women and children crept shyly out of the houses and sat around looking at her and talking among themselves. Two of the women touched her arm and chattered together. They examined her hair, rubbing it between their fingers and looking at it in amazement.

William explained, "They say they have never seen any hair like yours before and they want to know whether it is real. I told them it's real, and it's the prettiest hair I ever saw!" He grinned and went back to the conversation with the men.

One child came close and touched Julia's wristwatch and asked a question. Julia didn't understand him but thought he must be asking what it was. William explained to the child that, instead of looking to see where the sun was in the sky to show the time of day, the little round thing on Julia's arm could tell him what time of the day it was.

The wide-eyed child asked then, "Does it have a sun in it? I don't see a sun."

William laughed and said, "It has tiny wheels inside which move these straight pieces outside. They are called 'hands.' The watch is different from the sun because even at night, with no sun, the watch can tell us when the sun will come back again."

The child looked at William in confused disbelief.

In talking to William the old men used many gestures toward the women and children and Julia. She noticed that they pointed, not with their fingers, but by jutting their chins and lower lips out and throwing their heads backward. There were long, comfortable pauses in the conversation, while everyone just sat and looked at one another. Nobody was in a hurry. The women kept looking at Julia and then down at themselves. Julia realized one would have to live a long time among them, slowly winning their confidence, to understand them. William seemed to have been able to bridge the culture gap with the men to a good degree.

After about an hour, William said they must go. They waved their goodbyes and left, looking back and smiling at the women and children. But the two old men accompanied them over the trail as far as the waterfall, pointing out various sights to William. Julia simply followed along, as a woman in New Guinea is supposed to do.

Before parting, the old chief put his hand on William's shoulder and prayed a short prayer, looking up into the sky. William told Julia later that the chief had said, "O God living on top of the sky, we know your name is Jesus. Go with my friend and take care of him and save him from your enemies." It was a benediction. Then the two men, smiling their betel-nut smiles, faded back into the forest.

The two Australians meandered their way over the trail. Once more in the Land Rover, William chuckled. "What do you think the chief asked me?"

"I have no idea."

"He wanted to know if you were my wife. I told him no, but that it wasn't a bad idea. Then he said if I needed any shells or pigs to buy you with, he'd let me have them. And he hoped we'd have many children with hair like yours!"

"Well! You will never get me with shells and pigs, sir!" she exclaimed, then, "Who was that second man?"

"He was a former witch doctor."

"Former? A real kill 'em kind of witch doctor?"

"Definitely. Both the old chief and the witch doctor were converted about six years ago. Their lives have been drastically changed, causing a change in their whole tribe. The government's job of governing their tribe is much easier."

"How? Specifics, please."

"You see, the chief and the witch doctor were both very cruel. The chief himself had killed many of his enemies and kept his area in an uproar. Government officials were always wary of this part of the highlands because he was the most dreaded killer around. The witch doctor has been the cause of many other deaths by calling on evil spirits to kill people, or by putting a spell on people or by accusing them of something so that other warriors killed them. Now the witch doctor uses simple drugs he gets from the government and prays to God for his people to be healed. Many of his prayers have been answered and now people trust him."

"Oh, my goodness! A witch doctor and a cannibal chief! And those two were walking in the jungle with us!"

"Well, just be thankful that missionaries came some years ago! Since those two men are changed, so is their whole clan. Because they were natural leaders, government officials have given them responsibility in keeping order among their own tribe. They do a good job and say they are happy Christians. Didn't you think they looked happy?"

"Yes, thank the Lord! I wish they would stop chewing betel-nut and start using toothbrushes though!"

That night, stretching her tired legs, wearing a granny nightgown and heavy socks in order to keep warm in her cold bed, Julia laughed to herself. She was thinking about how horrified Aunt Rosa would be if she knew that her niece had been walking in the jungle with former killers. She couldn't quite picture Aunt Rosa tripping over the mountain paths alongside brown men in billum drapes and tanket leaves. She was also tickled over what the chief had said—that he would give William enough shells and pigs to buy her with. She went to sleep giggling. She dreamed William was buying her from Aunt Rosa, who was flirting with the witch doctor while surrounded by pearl shells, pigs and cannibal chiefs.

Chapter 6

*O*ne day William brought a young girl to Julia and Mary's door. "Girls, meet Megia. She comes from a village half an hour's walk from here and she wants to work for you. I know her parents and they have agreed. She's willing to do anything she's told to do—wash your clothes, cook, sweep. She seems eager to learn and wants to go to the government school to learn English in the mornings and work for you in the afternoons. Would you like to hire her?"

"Would we!" they chorused. "We are tired of coping alone with that wood stove!"

Thus Julia's real education in New Guinea's ways began in earnest.

Megia helped a great deal. She learned from them how they liked things done, and in return she taught them many things. She learned to use the wood stove and cook other things besides sweet potatoes, her basic food. She learned to like their food. The bathroom with its flush toilet was a source of constant amazement to her. Sometimes she brought them *shesh*, large mushrooms which grew out over the mountains, and sometimes a fresh pineapple from a neighboring village. Since she was studying English, they helped her learn household terms. She eagerly absorbed everything, and Julia found great delight in being able to teach. So Julia spent an extra hour with her each evening after dinner.

Julia used some of the methods she'd learned at the University of Kentucky to teach grade school children, and Megia progressed so fast the government teacher told her Megia was at the top of the class. Because Megia could understand some English, they could teach her a variety of subjects.

She was astonished to learn that dirt and germs, not evil spirits, caused illness. They were certain she did not believe them at first. Hadn't she always been taught that evil spirits cause all manner of bad things? But some of her beliefs began to disappear. Among other things, she began to wash herself. Bulai people had always believed that if a woman submerged herself in water, she would die. Mary and Julia were thankful that Megia learned otherwise! Everyone who went to school had to wash; that was one entrance requirement. No teacher could endure being closed up with a classroom full of children day after day when those children were smeared daily with old pig fat and never washed! Megia had even been able to persuade her younger brothers and sisters to wash off the pig fat and go to school, too. She took them down to the mountain stream and dipped herself into the water to show them she wouldn't die.

Sometimes she took Mary and Julia on hikes over the weekend, and they slept in low, native grass houses, zipped up in their sleeping bags. She cooked kau-kau in hot ashes for them. She showed them much of the countryside around Bulai—a place like no other on earth—with cloud-covered mountains, racing streams, dense jungles, deep gorges and fascinating people.

Megia explained many Bulai customs, and through her explanations Julia began to understand Megia's race. Megia told how evil spirits reside in rocks and trees, in shadows and thunder and lightning. She explained how some people made a "love potion" out of insects, ginger, dye powder and blood from their own bodies to influence one person's love. Julia and Mary learned that although some people did make love potions, most people thought it was a "big sin" and as a result would expect to receive strong punishment, even death. She related a story of how one villager made such a potion and he himself died of "fire in his stomach."

She described to them the sing-sings, which, she said, are the most important events in anyone's life. Villagers practice singing and dancing for many days and even weeks before the real event. Then on the given date, perhaps one or two hundred people of one tribe or area paint their faces, decorate themselves with feathers, beads and shells and dance and sing all night around the sacred tree. The singing is a weird chant and the dance is a rhythmic, flatfooted stomping which shakes the ground. After the dance is over the feast begins. Many pigs are killed, maybe 30 or 40, and everyone except the women eat them.

"You mean," Julia exclaimed, "That the women have to do all the work of raising those pigs and then can't eat any of them?"

"Not at the sing-sing feast, Misis. That bad luck for women. At other times they eat. I always help to kill pigs at the sing-sing."

"Oh, Megia, you kill some of the pigs yourself?" Julia shuddered. "How could you?"

"Yes, Misis," she answered simply. "With a club."

"How do you dress for the sing-sing and feast?"

"Not like this. This dress only for government school. I put on only woven cane belt, strips of possum fur around arms, pearl shells and beads. I put piece of crescent pearl shell in my nose and red bird-of-paradise feathers in headpiece. That's all."

As she pictured Megia practicing her ancient customs in killing pigs for the feast, Julia realized Megia was wading with a bare foot in each of two different streams of time. And Julia wondered how long it would take the new current to claim her.

"How do your people cook all those pigs, Megia?"

"I show you. Like this, Misis." First she dug a small hole just to show the procedure, then laid a handful of sticks crisscross over the hole. She found a few stones and put them on top of the sticks. "Now," she explained, "we make plan like this. We make hole, put sticks, put stones, then we put pig on stones. Don't cut up pig, just put all together. Fire burns sticks. Then hot stones and pig fall down into hole. Then we cover up with more hot stones, after that leaves and then cover everything with layer of dirt. We put bamboo stick straight down into hole with hot stones. Drip water through bamboo. Water on hot stones makes 'ssssttt' and cook pig. We cook about four hours. Easy, see?"

"What do the men do most of the time?" Julia asked. "I always see women working in gardens and growing kau-kau and taking care of pigs and children."

"Oh, sometimes men work—but not much work. They must protect families. Old men do nothing but sit and talk. Sometimes they make arrow or spear. Women do garden work. Old men make a face at young people and new ideas."

"Just like they do in America and Australia!"

Megia showed them trails through the bush. She pointed out a kind of small nut which tasted like coconut. She explained how pigs have to sleep in houses with women and girls—men and boys sleep alone. "Women must sleep with pigs to protect them. Somebody might take 'em away pigs!"

"Well, if women and men don't sleep together at night, when do they ever make love with one another?"

"Oh, sometimes in the kau-kau gardens."

"I heard once," Mary said to Megia, "that sometimes, if a little pig has no mother, a woman will feed the pig her own milk, at her own breast. Is that true?"

Megia looked unbelieving at such a question. "Why, yes, Misis! If little pig have no mother, then little pig die. Woman have to give milk. Lotsa womans got too much milk for won baby!"

Julia grimaced. It was hard to feel important in a culture

in which the pig was so revered. She knew there was a law against a woman nursing a pig at her breast. But how could a government really stop it? Mr. Richards had said, "Of course there's a law against it. But we are quite certain when we see a little pig following a woman and whimpering like a baby, that woman has been nursing it. She's really its mother. Their pigs are precious to them."

Every day brought Julia and Mary some new understanding of the people of Bulai Valley. Every day was full of adventure and challenge.

William and Julia were hurrying toward William's house one Saturday afternoon. From the approaching mists they knew rain would soon be falling. They had planned to play Scrabble and listen to William's records, then she would have dinner with him.

"Remember," William asked Julia, "I told you about Sekiba's friend, Tiba, and about his death? For a long time after that, Sekiba was gloomy. But you should see how he's rejuvenated since Megia's arrival at your house! He's been singing in the kitchen and preening in front of the mirror. Yesterday he said, 'I gotta go onetime 'long market, Mastah.' So I mimicked him, 'Yes, I know. You always go onetime 'long market when Megia go by. Megia maybe see you?'"

Julia laughed. "What did he say?"

"Sekiba just grinned and said, 'Yes, Mastah!' I must say I've been relaxing in the atmosphere of joy in the kitchen. Megia's been a great influence on my house."

But when they arrived at William's house, Julia could see Sekiba's joy had not lasted. He was fuming, and he banged the pots around violently in the kitchen. Concentration on Scrabble words was difficult. At last William could stand it no longer. "Stop that racket!" he shouted. "What's the matter with you today, Sekiba?"

Sekiba stood in the doorway, his face a thundercloud.

"I been 'long see Megia Pappa."

"What for?"

"I wanta go 'long marry Megia." His scowl looked ferocious.

"So why are you so angry about that?"

"Megia Pappa put bride price too much high."

"How much is the bride price he asks?"

"One 'em cassowary, 12 pearl shells and 20 pigs!"

"One of those huge birds?" Julia inquired.

Sekiba nodded.

"How much does one cassowary cost?"

"Two hundred and forty dollahs, Misis. Megia Pappa know it too much. But Megia big, strong girl—hips good, wide. Megia Pappa say, 'Megia big—raise plenty baby, garden and pigs. Megia also know to read big books. She worth plenty much.' So Pappa put 'em big price."

"How much does all that come to?" William inquired.

"Altogedder kissim nearly 500 dollahs, Mastah." Sekiba returned to the kitchen and they saw him jam a stick of firewood viciously into the stove. He banged down the lid and grumbled darkly, "Megia Pappa better go 'long look out. Maybe Dewel get 'em."

Julia gasped.

William's reaction was instantaneous. He strode to the kitchen. "Now YOU look out, Sekiba. Don't you start any of that devil stuff around here. I absolutely forbid it. You let the devil and Megia's Pappa alone! If you want Megia, you save up your money and get her according to the custom. Understand that?"

Sekiba refused to look at him. "Yes, Mastah."

"Now calm down and don't make so much noise in this kitchen!"

"Yes, Mastah."

But the whole afternoon their Scrabble conjurings were punctuated with clatter.

William's work took him through the whole Bulai Valley,

sometimes not so far in miles, but it took days of trekking away from home base. He often exclaimed how good it was to get home again, to shed heavy hiking shoes and dirty clothes, shave and take a bath. His bucket of bath water was heated with an electric plunger. His stove had no water reservoir connected to it. After one such trek, he was having a relaxed dinner with Julia, Mary and Marvin. He had arrived late. He said that, because the electricity was temporarily off, he couldn't heat any bath water and had to wait an hour for it.

"Don't you sometimes miss the luxury of all the hot water you want, as you could have in Sydney?" Julia asked him.

"Well, I wouldn't mind a little extra hot water. But miss Sydney? No, especially not since you came, Julie." He stretched and tried to relax in the small wicker chair. The chair was not comfortable and his legs were too long. He put his hand over Julia's on the table. "My greatest luxury is just being near you."

Mary and Marvin grinned at them. "Would you like for us to leave?"

William looked at Julia and answered Marvin, "Not necessarily, not unless you object to hearing how sweet I think Julie is."

Julia broke in. "William is a real ego-inflater!"

William continued. "I congratulate you girls on the fine Australian dinner, so far from Australia. You've been here about 10 months now, right? I'm happy to see that the days of lopsided cakes and unpalatable whatever-it-might-have-beens are gone. Between you girls and Megia, life is worth living around here!"

Julia made a face at him. "No thanks to you! You haven't been around here enough lately to see that we get decent, dry firewood. Next time I'm going to give you a smoked omelet and see how you like it. Everything we've eaten lately has been smoke-flavored because of that old wet wood. It's beginning to be our favorite flavor."

"New load of dry firewood coming up tomorrow. Honest!"

"I'm just full of news tonight," said Julia, "and this is the best ever. Have you heard how Megia took things into her own hands and probably started the beginning of the end of the Pappa-knows-best society around here?"

"No."

Marvin broke in. "She is upsetting the status quo of her clan! It's given the pig-watching ladies something to gossip about, and Bulai will never be the same again when this word gets around!"

"What in the world did she do?" William asked and lightly tugged Julia's chair a little closer to his own.

"Well," Julia related, "this is classic, and I bet it never happened before. The other day Megia said, 'Misis, you got plenty money me to borrow?' Then she astounded me by saying, 'I wanta go 'long borrow 200 dollahs!'"

"Two hundred dollars?" William was as amazed as Julia had been.

"Yes, William. I asked her what she was going to do with all that money and she stunned me again by announcing, 'I gonna pay my Pappa big bride price.'

"I couldn't believe it. I argued with her, 'But Megia, girls don't pay their own bride price. Their husbands pay for them.'

"But Megia was stubborn and said, 'Sekiba, he want me. My Pappa set price too much high. Sekiba he got 'em 300 dollahs. So I tell 'em Sekiba I borrow 200 dollahs from Misis and take all his money too and pay my Pappa.'"

William's eyebrows shot up. "This *is* new Bulai society! Did you lend her the money?"

"Well, I didn't want to break up her whole social system, so I talked it over with Grant first. He said it was certainly a new idea around here, but if Megia's father would accept it, perhaps it was worth a try. So I loaned her the money. The next day Megia came in all smiles. She reported there hadn't been any explosion in her father's pit-pit house. All that money was too tempting to Pappa.

"Megia said, 'I tell my Pappa—I give you this 500 dollahs, so now Megia buy Megia! Pappa no more boss man. Pappa tell Megia nothing what to do. If Megia wanta marry Sekiba, Pappa no talk-talk. If Megia don't wanta marry nobody, Pappa no talk-talk. *Megia bilong Megia!*'"

Julia giggled. "And you know, her pappa was stupefied. He sat for an hour and chewed on his betel-nut over the new ultimatum, and he didn't say a single word. He finally just stuck out his hand and took the 500 dollars!"

William threw back his head and laughed. "Well, that girl's got real spunk. Looks like we'll have a wedding soon."

"Looks like it."

William jumped up and pulled Julia to her feet. "Get your coat, Red. Moon's beautiful tonight; let's take a walk."

"Haven't you walked enough today?"

"Not with you."

"Don't you need a chaperon?" Mary asked, grinning.

"I think Marvin would like you to stay with him. He looks lonesome," William said with a smile as he opened the door.

They ambled down the winding road toward the airstrip, lightly holding hands. A fat, golden moon hovered just over the top of the highest Bulai ridge, slanting glowing fingers down the slopes. William put his arm around her.

"Hi, Mr. William Banner, terror with women!" Julia said, her eyes meeting his.

"Hi, Red. Know something? In one more month you'll be going back to Australia for your month's leave, and I don't want you to go at all."

"Oh, you'll survive. You did before I came."

"That was before you came! Things are different now." He stopped, turned Julia toward him and held her close. "You know I love you, Julie. Marry me and don't go. Wait until we both can go."

She sighed. "Oh, William, it's a temptation because

you're the most wonderful man I've ever known—in every way you're wonderful. I've seen this coming too, and I — "

"Didn't you want me to say it?"

Julia looked up. Her eyes were level with his chin. "It isn't that I don't want you to say it, but I haven't known how to answer you. I have to be fair and truthful. I love you and respect you very much. But I can't honestly say I'm *in love* with you. There must be a difference. Seems like when you're in love, fireworks ought to pop off, or rockets explode or something!"

He leaned down, rubbed his cheek against hers and asked, "You mean you don't hear those fireworks and rockets? Why Julie, when I kiss you I can't hear anything else!" He kissed her gently.

She felt so secure in his arms as she returned the kiss, but she didn't hear any fireworks. "Please, William, let me go to Australia. I need a change after a year here, and I've been looking forward to a holiday. When I get back, there will be an answer for you. Maybe I'll miss you so much that fireworks will explode when I see you again."

"Well, I'm going to explode those fireworks one way or another. Promise to think about me in Sydney?"

"I promise. Oh, William, I really want to fall madly in love with you! I know I'll never find anybody greater!"

"I want you to fall madly in love with me, Julie. I hope you realize you are so much in love with me that you'll come back a week early. I've never wanted to marry anyone before, but I do want you."

The next Saturday afternoon, he rapped on Julia's door. She opened it and stuck her head out. "Whatever it is, we don't want any!"

Julia saw his eyes light up as he looked at her, even though she was wearing a tacky old blue sweater and skirt. "I've an errand to do in an office about 16 miles out," he said after greeting her. "It will probably be our last Saturday together before you go to Sydney. Come with me in the Land Rover?"

She smiled at his eager eyes and the way the sun shone on his tousled, brown hair. She wondered whether to enjoy being near someone meant you were in love with him. Or was she just feeling happy for no reason? "Can't."

"You can't? Why not?"

She tried to look serious. "I'm pig-sitting!"

"You're *what*?"

She shrugged. "Pig-sitting." She said it casually as if it were an everyday occurrence for her. "You see," she explained as to a five-year-old, "Megia got a bargain today and bought three new baby pigs. Their mother had died. Megia intends them to be a wedding present for Sekiba. Then Megia's father asked her to go on an errand with her brother to the next village. She couldn't possibly be home before dark. She didn't want her father and mother to know about the baby pigs, and she couldn't carry all three of them there and back."

Julia stopped, leaned against the door and laughed at William's look of incredulity. "Don't let your mouth hang open so far. It might lock in that position! Anyway, these baby pigs have to be fed every two hours with a bottle of warm milk. So I told Megia to go on her errand, so—" she waved her hand over toward a corner where three baby pigs were rolling around in a large box, "I'm pig-sitting for the afternoon!"

William leaned against the door laughing. "Pig-sitting is the craziest reason I ever heard of to refuse a date. Okay, my little swineherd friend, *my* errand can wait. If you have to pig-sit, *I* have to pig-sit! I'll even help you feed them when it's time. Meanwhile, I'll beat you at Scrabble."

"Come in, sir. I can use some help. They all want to eat at once. I think they're cute!"

She never spent a more hilarious afternoon in her whole life.

Chapter 7

Julia's first year was soon over and she was leaving Bulai for four weeks in Sydney. She felt a definite lonely twinge as the little plane circled up out of the valley and headed toward Port Moresby, leaving William and Mary waving to her. She thought about everything she had experienced and learned since last year. Her horizons had certainly been broadened in a year!

But when, hours later, the panorama of red-tiled roofs which was Sydney spread out under her approaching jet, she realized she was eager for a month in civilization.

Aunt Rosa met her at the airport airily talking a streak as usual. It was as if she had been talking ever since Julia left and hadn't noticed her absence. Aunt Rosa looked older, and seemed a little more desperate to hide increasing wrinkles under her expensive makeup. She had always been a bit vague about some things, but she was never vague about herself or men.

"Oh, Julia, it's nice to have you home!" She looked her niece up and down. "We'll have to do something about your clothes. They're rather - er - worn, don't you think? And your skirts are just way out of date, my dear! Skirts are short, you know!" She laughed a tinkling, up-and-down-the-scale trill.

"You shouldn't ever worry about short dresses, Aunt Rosa. Your legs are good enough to wear them."

Aunt Rosa glanced appreciatively at her shapely legs, moving her ankle from side to side for a better view. "Why, thank you, dear. And tell me, how was New Guinea? Was it really wild? Aren't you too thin? Wasn't the food any good?" Without waiting for any kind of answer she burbled on, "I'm having a welcome-home dinner for you tomorrow night. You just *must* go shopping tomorrow for a new gown. I've got the most divine man I want you to meet. I told you about him in a letter."

"Oh, Aunt Rosa," Julia remonstrated when she could get a word in. "Are you sure he isn't another new boyfriend of *yours*?"

Aunt Rosa trilled again. "Oh, dear, no, not mine. I wish I were young enough for him. He's divine, I tell you, divine! And he's just right for you!"

Julia was busy looking out both sides of the taxi window, watching Sydney rush past. "Oh, it's good to be home again! Who's the new man?"

"He's great, I tell you, just perfect! His name is Graham Moresby of *the* Moresby family, and he's a lawyer."

"Graham Moresby-hmmm-that rings a bell, but there are lots of Moresbys probably. Are you sure he's not a stuffed shirt?"

"No indeed! He's all man. You just wait. Besides being such a perfect man, he's intellectual, rich, interesting, a bachelor and seven years older than you, Julia. He's just right!"

Aunt Rosa was quite famous in Sydney society for both her house and her cuisine. The next evening she gave one of her perfect little dinner parties at home, which was one of the better "old terraced houses of Sydney." Her whole house was furnished in Louis XV. It just suited her tinkling laugh.

Twelve guests in evening finery gathered in Aunt Rosa's living room. Julia, her back to the door, happened to be in conversation with a young woman who was dressed in a bare-shoulder, glittering black dress. The woman looked beyond Julia and her face suddenly glowed. Julia turned to note the reason for the transformation, and then she saw him. Undoubtedly, he was the most perfect specimen of manhood she'd ever seen. He had arrived fashionably late and made an entrance that every female in the room under 75 silently applauded.

Six feet, three inches, broad shouldered, black wavy hair and bright blue eyes, he stood taller than anyone else in the room. His eyes searched for his hostess, and when he saw Aunt Rosa, he walked toward her. "Good evening, Rosa. I'm delighted you asked me to come."

Aunt Rosa had Julia by the arm. "Graham, I'd like you to meet my niece, Julia Harrell. She's just come from working in New Guinea. Julia, this is Graham Moresby."

Julia looked way up and smiled.

Graham's square jaw was softened by the perfect cleft in his chin. "How nice to meet you, Miss Harrell!" When he smiled down at her he was almost *too* handsome. "Your aunt sang your praises when she asked me to dinner tonight. Looks like she was in the right key."

"Don't believe that tune!" Julia hoped he found her beautiful in her soft orange dress. And she hoped he liked red hair. Suddenly, it mattered a great deal to her what he thought.

He looked at her, appraising every detail of her appearance.

Julia felt quite conspicuous. Her father used to look at racehorses like that.

He nodded approval. "I didn't know redheads could look so beautiful in orange."

"Maybe I'm just more daring than the rest."

His black eyebrows lifted. "Maybe."

She wondered whether, in his opinion, she'd scored one or lost one.

But he went on, "Anyway, please don't talk to anyone else tonight. I want you all to myself, and I want to hear all about New Guinea."

"You probably wouldn't believe it if I told you!" Why in

the world was she so snappy tonight? Especially when she was trying to impress him.

Whether he was interested in hearing about New Guinea or not, she couldn't be sure. Seated beside him at the table, he asked her questions but she wondered whether he was really listening when she answered. His attention seemed to wander a bit. But he focused on her when he talked about himself, so she tried to be a good listener. He was making the impression!

Later she thought she must have done *something* right, for the next four weeks they were together as much of the time as he could be out of his office. "They're going to fire me if I don't stay in the office and do some work," he remarked one day. "But I've told them that rich old Uncle Harry's will and flirty Mrs. Downey's divorce can wait. I've got only a month to know this girl!"

Julia looked sidelong under her lashes at him. She was thrilled to be with him, but she didn't want to go totally overboard. This wasn't the first time he'd made such a remark. Either he was teasing, or he was making quick hay. "Maybe if you had more time you wouldn't be interested in knowing this girl."

"I mean it," he insisted. "I've never met anyone like you before, Julia. At least not anyone who's as refreshing. You're so honest, so wholesome."

"So is a lump of dough!"

"Don't compare yourself to a lump of dough! It's been a year since you were in Sydney. Let me show it to you."

And so he showed her, from one end of the sprawling city to the other and back again. St. Mary's, which had inspired the song, "The Bells of St. Mary's," the bay areas, beaches, Harbour Bridge, Circular Quay, the opera house, the picturesque boulders called "The Heads" overlooking the sea, the fort referred to as "Pinch-gut," the "Mrs. McQuarie" places, Queen's Square, King's Cross with its "fringe people," the Gap, Spit Bridge, Whale Beach, The Point, Palm

Beach, the churches and on over the city they went. They also drove out to the famous blowhole and Kangaroo valley. Places came alive once more for Julia, many which she hadn't seen since childhood.

Seeing Sydney with Graham was thrilling. It was so good to be admired, to meet Graham's wealthy friends, to drive on smooth streets in Graham's American car. It was quite a jump from a tenant house on a horse farm in Kentucky to the society column in the Sydney paper. It was a greater leap from the pig-oriented society in New Guinea to a pleasure-oriented aristocracy in Australia.

One week couldn't have vanished already!

Julia hardly saw Aunt Rosa, but one morning as they passed in the hall, both dressed to go out, Aunt Rosa called, "Didn't I tell you he's divine?"

"Yes, and I need wings to keep up with him. You were right though—he's everything a girl could wish for!"

One day melted into another. It was usually so late when Julia came in that she fell asleep almost instantly. But two nights before her leave was over, sleep wouldn't come. Graham had kissed her more passionately that night than before, a long, lingering good-night. She thought she heard some fireworks and anticipation arose.

And now in bed with the light turned off, she was too excited to sleep, and her foot began to itch. Somehow in the gossamer region of reverie, black hair and blue eyes got all tangled up with brown hair and brown eyes. The moon over Sydney harbor had drifted and was brooding over Bulai. A long car had somehow bumped into a dusty Land Rover. Julia snapped upright. She hadn't thought about William for a whole week!

She slid back down into the bed and began to wonder what that meant. She *hadn't* thought about him for a week. That ought to be some kind of answer to William's proposal.

Idly scratching her foot, she began to giggle, remembering the last Saturday afternoon when William had come to pig-sit with her. What fun they'd had feeding the baby pigs—and his hands were as gentle with them as hers. And he had beaten her at Scrabble. Lying there, she had to confess to herself that there had never been anyone she could feel so completely at home with, nor as contented with, as William. They both liked the same kind of music, the same kind of food, the same kind of books. They could be silly together. Their silences could be long and still be comfortable. They could discuss their feelings with great honesty as they talked about God and the serious things of life. He had confided one day, "I have realized that one important thing for me to do with my life is to help this country and people progress. And," he had looked straight at Julia, "the other most important thing in my life is you, Red. I've never loved anyone as I love you."

She felt good now remembering it. And Graham, how did Graham make her feel? Graham flattered her. He was an exciting man and made her feel like an exciting and desirable woman. She admitted a little watchful awareness with Graham though, a feeling that she ought to be constantly on her toes; that he was a lot to live up to. There was always the fear she might wear the wrong clothes or say the wrong thing, and that Graham would be embarrassed because of her. Then she began to seriously talk to herself. *Graham is extremely attractive to women, and I'm not really beautiful. I know I'm not, no matter what William says. Wonder what Graham sees in me? Does he love me?*

Graham's always able to get the best tickets to everything, the best seats in restaurants. But I have to admit that sometimes he seems a little pompous. He like to make an impression. Maybe that's because he's interested in politics. And maybe I notice it because I'm used to William's casual, easy way, as if being with me is the most natural thing in the world. He's never tried to impress me.

She sat up and leaned against a propped up pillow and asked herself aloud, "Okay, Julia Harrell, be honest now.

What do you really think of Graham? Are you in love with him?"

I must be. It feels great to move in his social circles. I feel important. He opens so many doors; any girl would be thrilled.

"Anything you don't like about him? You've seen him nearly every day for a month now."

W-e-l-l, sometimes I have had a twinge of resentment at the way Graham introduces me as "my little friend from the jungles of New Guinea," as if I were some rare specimen. I don't care to be known as a "little jungle girl." Makes me feel inadequate.

"What do you and Graham talk about?"

Oh, about parties, clothes, gossip, food. I guess we haven't talked about anything serious. Not about feelings or inside things that really matter. She sighed. *But I think Graham's in love with me, and he'll ask me to marry him before I go.* Visions of herself as Graham's wife flickered across the ceiling—elegant house, clothes, cars, beautiful children, a leading society matron. In short, everything any woman could want. All that and handsome Graham, too! Aunt Rosa would be so fluttered she'd just fly away! Julia giggled, scratched her foot, wiggled her toes in the wide, luxurious bed and finally fell asleep.

The next two days flew by and she was dressing for her last date with Graham before returning to New Guinea. *Tonight he'll ask me!* she confided to herself in the mirror. Tonight was to be an intimate candlelight dinner in Sydney's famous high, revolving restaurant. From that height, all the colored lights of Sydney and the harbor would be dainty fairy wands splashed in rainbow colors.

But during the intimate, candle-lit dinner, the talk never became personal. He spoke of his work as a lawyer, his involvement in politics. Julia knew he was handsomely paid by his clients at the top of the social ladder and was always in demand as an eligible bachelor at dinners. He was at home in a world foreign to her, but as his wife, she was sure he would help her fit in. But no words were spoken of feelings and futures. After the great rush he'd given her, she was more than a little baffled. *He'll say something after dinner on the way home. He knows I have to leave tomorrow.*

But Graham took her back to Aunt Rosa's house and kissed her, a long, hard kiss. "Thank you, Julia, for spending all your vacation time with me. I've enjoyed every minute of it."

"I've loved it, too."

"Have a good year in New Guinea, love, and don't forget to write. I'll write to you." There was not even a promise to see her off at the airport the next day.

Julia waited at the door and watched his car pull away. *And that is that!* She closed the door in disbelief. *Is that all?*

Still stunned the next day, she felt like a zombie boarding the plane for New Guinea.

William took Julia's bag, swung her down from the plane and kissed her eagerly. "Hi, Julie. I sure missed you!"

She managed to smile at him, noting the lock of brown hair still falling over his eye.

"Tell me now, what did you do in Sydney? Did you remember me? Did you find a new boyfriend? If you did, I'll shoot him! I'll bet they were standing in line to welcome you home." If he noticed her silence, he gave no indication. Julia felt dazed, almost as if someone else were walking in her shoes.

The next two months were as if she'd never been away, except for a pain in her middle. *Must be my heart hurting— no, maybe the people in Bulai are right, maybe love is in the lungs. It does hurt to breathe.* She was confused—she'd been so sure Graham was in love with her. She was aware of William's effort to cheer her up. Was it her imagination that he suspected something?

One afternoon William came by the office. "Come on,

Julie. I've had Sekiba pack a supper for us. Let's go climb a mountain."

Anything, something to do! "Okay, wait till I get my magic climbing shoes on!" She was proud of herself for sounding light.

They climbed the hill to his favorite spot and sat gazing on the ever-changing scene. The whole Bulai Valley ringed around, above and below in green and gold with blue and purple shadows. She remembered the first time she had climbed up with William, a year before. It seemed like a century.

They sat watching rays of the sun creep off the valley floor, and the shadows begin to settle. He asked gently, "Like to tell me about it?"

"What?" She knew what.

"Whatever it is that's hurting you." He waited, not looking at her. Then, "Did you fall in love in Sydney?"

She sighed a deep sigh. "I think so."

"Do I know him?" William's mouth was grim.

"You won't believe this, William. It's Graham Moresby."

"Graham Moresby!" Now he *was* grim. "Tell me about him."

So Julia told him everything. She couldn't help it that William was so easy to talk to, and she ended up in tears, her head on his shoulder. "I just don't understand. I was sure he was falling in love with me. And for the first time I think I'm in love. Oh, William, I'm so sorry. It should have been you!"

"Moresby's an absolute idiot! How could he be so stupid?" he asked, holding her close. "I always gave him credit for more sense than that, even if I didn't like him. Any fool that would let you get away—"

Julia sat up and sniffed. "Well, I suppose it was just me. I was fresh from New Guinea and had simply forgotten how the social rat race is run. It probably didn't mean anything to him; no doubt he romances a lot of girls and I was just a dazzled, dumb, red-headed jungle girl!"

"Stop downgrading yourself! Stop crying and eat your sandwiches. You know what? Now you and I belong to the same club. I'm in love with you and you're in love with Moresby. We can be sad together, and you can weep on Uncle William's shoulder anytime you need to. You know," he put his finger under her chin, "I think you're so sweet, I'd even *give* you Moresby if that would make you happy. Of course, I might grind him up first!"

"Oh, you're crazy!" Julia felt better because she would never have to pretend with William. "Come on, it's time to go home. Rain's coming."

Waiting for her at home was a note from Grant Richards: Julia: Received a radio message from a Mr. Graham Moresby in Sydney. He asked me to grant you an additional two days' leave. He also requested you meet him in Port Moresby at 11 a.m. this Saturday, the 24th. He has booked two rooms at the Gateway Hotel. He says it's urgent. You have my permission to go to Port Moresby on Friday. —Grant Richards.

Julia read it, unbelieving, a second time. Then the floods of joy came. *This must be what surfing feels like, riding my own private wave of happiness. I was right! I knew it! Graham does love me or he wouldn't do this!*

She tried to ignore the stricken look on William's face the next day when she showed him the note.

"All the best, Julie. I'm still here if you need me." He walked away, his shoulders hunched.

The jet from Sydney shrieked smoothly to a stop in front of the Port Moresby terminal and Graham was the third one out. He leaned over the visitors' fence and ignored the customs officials long enough to kiss her soundly.

When he was finished with customs, they sat in the garden of the Gateway Hotel overlooking the sea. She waited for him to speak. She would take her cues from him.

"Well, Julia, you did it."

"I did?" How handsome he was! Tall, taller than William.

Beautiful, strong, even teeth, broad shoulders, black hair perfectly groomed.

"Yes, you did. I intended to take my own time about falling in love, and had planned I would eventually do it after I was firmly established in law. I wanted to make a good reputation for myself and being promised to one person wasn't part of the plan. I thought it was better to be the 'desirable bachelor.' I would be asked to lots of places, meet all the right people in society, be on my own and not responsible to anyone."

He stirred his lemon squash and finished it off. "When I let you come back to New Guinea, I was really testing myself. I had to see how it was without you. Now I know. I don't want to be without you, Julia, I want to marry you. Will you? I'm very much in love with you."

Blinking away tears of joy, she burbled, "I thought you'd never ask! That's not very original, I know, but I thought you never would!" She sounded just like Aunt Rosa.

"I have considered this from every angle," he went on. "The family approves of you because they know your aunt. I can picture you in my life becoming the mother of my children, presiding over my house and taking your place in Sydney society. You have an adaptability which will help you do all those things well. And I love you. Will you?"

"Of course I will." Just like that!

He leaned over and kissed her. "On the hope that you would say yes, I brought this." He reached into his pocket and produced a small box. It looked old. He opened the lid and there, nestled in a bed of blue velvet, was a ring with one large, perfectly formed, translucent pearl. She had never seen such a beautiful gem before. "Oh, it's gorgeous!" she gasped. "It takes my breath away! Is it really for me?"

"Yes, and it has a history behind it."

Julia didn't tell him she already knew something of its history.

"An ancestor of mine got it from a native on Warrior Island, early in 1860. The story goes that he found an abundance of pearls there, but this one was the real gem, the largest and most perfect. It has been the engagement ring of our line of Moresby ladies ever since. I had a tough time talking my mother out of it, but she knows that's part of the legacy. A Moresby mother must always give it up for her son's engagement. Do you like it?"

Julia was amazed, just looking at it. "Like it? Oh, Graham, it's even a sacrilege to ask if I like it. It's almost as if you were asking whether I like an angel. It's so perfect!"

He slipped it on her finger. "You are now a Moresby lady."

In a flash of memory she heard William saying, "I always did envy the Moresby's their pearl." But why did she have to think about William at that moment?

Graham brought her back. "You're dreaming, darling. But as I told you, you will have to promise to give it up when our son wants it for his engagement."

"I will not! If he intends to take this away from me, I just won't have any sons!" She laughed at his look of surprise.

"We have only two days together here, so let's make some plans. When will you marry me?"

Julia sighed and scratched her foot. "Oh, Graham, I'd like to right now. But I've signed a contract with this company for two years, and I still have nine months to go. If I left now, Mr. Richards would be in an awful hole. He really needs me."

"Nine months! I don't like that. But our family will want a large wedding and plans will have to be made for that. Will you trust us in Sydney with the arrangements? I told your Aunt Rosa I was going to ask you, and she is ecstatic. I've heard women say it takes a long time to plan a big wedding."

"But I don't care about a big wedding."

"Well, but society . . . uh, Moresby tradition, you know."

So they made tentative plans for a late August wedding, about nine months away. They hired a car and drove all over Port Moresby's hills overlooking the sea. They explored old World War II bunkers, investigated the Government House and the museum, tramped through Koki's native market, searched out Sogeri with its rubber plantations, took out a boat and surveyed the native village built over water on stilts and the sunken wreck of the "MacDuhi," bombed and run aground on the reef during the war.

They stopped to watch three old men carving with hatchets on what would be a totem pole. One other ancient man sat in the shade and gave orders in a raspy voice. No doubt he was the greatest authority on totem carving.

The two days ended too soon, and Graham kissed her a tender goodbye. "So sorry to leave you, darling. Write to me often because I'll have to be satisfied with letters. We'll make plans in Sydney for our wedding. I love you."

Julia waved as his jet taxied out; then boarded the small Papuan Air Lines plane for the flight back to Bulai. As her plane circled for a landing, she looked down at the now familiar scene of the Bulai Valley. It felt like home.

"Where's William?" she asked Mary who met her in a company Land Rover.

"He had to go to Lae on business. He should be back tomorrow." Mary's eyes widened as she saw the magnificent pearl on Julia's finger. "So he *did* ask you! I'd marry anybody, young or old, who'd put a ring like that on *my* finger!"

"Yeah, yeah," Julia jeered, knowing Mary didn't mean a word of that last comment. "You know perfectly well you can't see anybody but Marvin, and he's a missionary. Poor at that!"

"You're right, and I love him, poverty and all, and I'll probably get him and no pearl at all," Mary agreed cheerfully.

William came back the next day, and Julia saw him from the office window. He didn't stick his head in the door and say hello as usual, but he was finally there to walk home with her from the office at closing time. He whistled when he saw her ring, but his manner was subdued. "So that's the pearl I've always envied Moresby for. Never saw it close before. Well, no doubt it's a beautiful insurance policy," he said, holding Julia's hand longer than necessary. "But, know what?" He pushed the brown hair out of his eyes. "Bulai has been a warrior valley for centuries, and you're the prettiest pearl in it, even when you're soaking wet in the rain! You're prettier than Moresby's pearl, and I'd rather have you. He's certainly lucky to have both."

"William, I—"

But he interrupted her. There was no twinkle in his brown eyes. "Okay, so you've promised to marry Moresby. I'll shoot square. I still want to be your friend, so I'll promise not to tell you I love you anymore, at least not every day. Why," he brightened, "you might even begin to miss hearing me say it. Yep, from now on, you're my good friend, Red. Honest, I'll keep it that way. I gracefully lose. Shake on it?"

She solemnly shook hands with him and wondered at the tears that suddenly stung her eyes.

Days merged into weeks, punctuated with stacks of office typing, short notes from Aunt Rosa with material swatches and letters from Graham filled with wedding plans and love. He quoted his mother's ideas often. "Mother says, since your own mother is gone, you'll probably be interested in this idea . . . "; and, "Aunt Rosa is sending you samples of materials for bridesmaids' dresses . . . ."

Being too far away to have many good ideas about her own wedding, of course she was grateful for all the help she could get. Sometimes she thought she must be dreaming. Sydney and Graham often seemed remote. He wrote of his encounters with people in Sydney, where he went, what he did: golf, sailing, games, parties and tactics he used to win divorces for playful married couples. His life was a million miles away from Julia's quiet valley.

Sometimes she even resented her own efforts to help build a more meaningful life for the Bulai people. At this distance, though, Sydney society seemed valueless and empty. At times she envied Graham's luxurious life, at the same time she mentally criticized him for living a life devoid of real meaning.

She remembered some of the things he'd said at Port Moresby and she couldn't help but feel he sounded like a stuffed shirt. "The Moresby's tradition." "Now you are a Moresby lady." She felt that parties, boat rides, games and operas were just playing at life. Here, Bulai people struggled with poverty, disease, evil spirits and witchcraft. Immersed in Bulai problems, she often wondered whether readjustment to Sydney could ever be possible. The contrast seemed too great.

She was alternately elated, depressed and increasingly restless. Time began to drag. William was gone much of the time, probably by design, and she missed the easy camaraderie they'd once enjoyed. He was distant and guarded when he was near, and she admitted to herself she missed hearing his breezy, "You're cute, Red," or, "I love you; don't forget me Julie!"

Well, her choice was made, and she'd just have to survive until the year was over and she was back with Graham. Mrs. Graham Moresby! *The* Mrs. Graham Moresby, red-haired society matron. Matron of the pearl! And never any more pig-sitting!

One day Megia said, "Two misis come church Sunday, maybe! Megia and Sekiba gonna be baptized."

"Really, Megia?"

"Yes. Me want go 'long be Christian. Sekiba, 'em too. Old ways too much no good. We already had lessons from God's talk Book. We both believe Jesus."

On Sunday both Mary and Julia went with Megia to the small pit-pit church on the hill. William came in with Sekiba and sat on the men's side. The congregation began by singing a New Guinean tune. They sang with spirit and their souls "swung along" as they enjoyed the singing. But later when they attempted to sing a translated English tune, their singing was flat and uninspired. They certainly sang their own tunes in their own short scale best. Julia did not care for their type of music, it would take years to develop a liking for it.

She could partly understand the prayers and sermon in the Bulai language. Looking over the congregation sitting cross-legged on mats on the floor, she was amused to see a few small pigs and chickens among the women and children. Pigs and chickens in church? She giggled and whispered to Mary, "Wonder how much the pigs get out of the sermon?"

"More than you will if you don't keep quiet!" Mary retorted.

Julia was touched by the simplicity of the baptism and moved by the solemnity of the couple's first Communion. She noticed the Communion elements were sweet potatoes and water.

As they walked down the hill after the service, a Bulai man was standing on a nearby hillside, shouting and shaking his spear. His greased body glistened, and his white-feather headdress vibrated in anger. Beside him stood several clan members, also brandishing spears. Sekiba and Megia stopped in the road and listened for a few moments. Megia stood with her hands on her hips and shouted a defiant reply. "Megia baptized because of God's talk. I not afraid evil spirits any-more. Megia and Sekiba now Christian and will only do what God's talk say. Don't bother me no more!"

"What's all that shouting about, Megia?"

"Chief very angry at baptism. Says no good thing for our clan. But I not afraid. God's talk way better way!"

Megia and Sekiba walked on, and William caught up with Julia. "I'm puzzled over something, William. When they served the Communion elements to Megia and Sekiba, they didn't serve the usual bread and wine, did they?"

"No. The Communion elements here are sweet potatoes and water. That's what the people in New Guinea know, and in most places in the highlands, it's the only thing available. Who has bread and wine out here?"

"I just never thought about it before. Somehow I always had the idea that without bread and wine there couldn't be Communion."

"Well, that isn't the way New Guinea people feel. And I've heard that in villages in India they serve *chappatties* and raisin juice!"

"What are chappatties?"

"Flat bread made out of wheat flour and water." They walked in silence for a while. "I heard a story once," he chuckled, "about a minister here in New Guinea who used to serve quinine tablets and water for Communion."

"Quinine tablets?"

"Yes. He realized it did two things: it served for Communion as well as bread and wine, and it helped to guard the communicants from malaria. People soon found out that quinine produced a buzzing in the ears and somehow got the notion that the buzzing meant they were probably filled with the Holy Spirit. Well, they wanted to be filled with the Holy Spirit, so at Communion they used to swallow as many quinine pills as they could, and also snitch some to take home with them. I won't vouch for the truth of that story!"

Julia laughed. "You're just full of information today!"

Sekiba and Megia wanted to be married in the church. And Megia announced she was not going to allow herself to be smeared with the usual mixture of oil and charcoal which was expected of every bride. "Thatsa no good practice, and Sekiba wanta no black wife!"

Mary and Julia spent many evenings making a long, white dress for Megia, the first wedding dress of its kind in Bulai. Mary had a portable sewing machine. Julia had asked Aunt Rosa to send a white slip, six yards of filmy white material and some net and sew-on bands of pearls for the veil. Mary was a better seamstress than Julia, but between them they produced a masterpiece. Megia was enchanted.

When the dress was ready, everyone in Bulai was invited to the church for the wedding. "Come when the sun is straight up above your heads," at noon. But the church was crowded long before that. Sekiba went in wearing new white pants and shirt which William had bought for him in Port Moresby. Sekiba sat patiently on the floor mat by the pulpit table, waiting for Megia.

Megia put on her new dress and veil, pearl-shell necklace (a gift from Sekiba), flowers in her hair, and she was ready. When she walked into the tiny, hillside grass church with its metal roof, the crowd moaned in approval. Sekiba jumped up, his eyes open wide.

They stood before a missionary and their own people. East and West combined to bring these two young people together. Most people in Bulai had never seen a Christian wedding, and certainly no other bride and groom were arrayed in such finery. With every question and answer, the audience softly moaned in answer too. After the "Amen," Sekiba grinned and said to the audience, "Sekiba get 'im pine wife!"

They disappeared happily into their new thatched-roof pit-pit house.

Chapter 8

A few weeks later, Julia was in bed with a cold and missed three days of work. On the third afternoon, she sat propped up on a steel folding chair in the living room. She wore a heavy bathrobe, a white cloth reeking of eucalyptus oil around her neck, and long wool socks on her feet.

William knocked on the door and poked his head in. "Hi, Red! Heard you were sick. Need some cheering up?"

"I certainly do," Julia retorted, her voice sounding like a foghorn. "It's been ages since you've been over and I've missed you!"

His face lit up. "Now that's the most inspiring and stimulating bit of news I've heard since you came home with that big insurance policy on your finger!"

She looked steadily at him through watery eyes.

"Okay, okay. I remember. No declarations. So, we'll talk. How've you been, besides this cold, I mean?"

"Oh, so-so. I'm getting restless. Can't you tell me any news—or any stories?" She sounded like a petulant child.

He leaned back in a chair and stretched his long legs. "Okay, well, once upon a time there was this stinkin' old step-mother—"

"Oh, William, you're crazy!" She laughed and had a coughing spasm.

He sat quietly for a while.

"What are you thinking?" Julia asked.

"Well, once in a while I do have a serious thought, and I've been thinking lately about personal sacrifices. Julie, did you ever consider spending the rest of your life out here, helping Bulai people?"

"Not me! Life is too formidable out here. There's nothing at all gentle about these highlands. It's as if a giant shovel had strip-mined the earth and piled up the mountains, and nobody thought to plant any trees on most of them. Everything's jagged and difficult."

William now looked straight at her. "Afraid of difficulties?"

She squirmed. "No but, well, maybe I am. I guess I'd rather have an . . . an insulated life."

He pondered. "Yes, I've sometimes longed for an insulated life, too. But I realize that insulation is often *isolation*. And in isolating ourselves from hardships, we isolate ourselves from striving. And if we don't have to strive, we deny ourselves the joy and pride of achieving."

"I didn't know you were so philosophical!" The conversation was making her uncomfortable, and she was already uncomfortable enough with the cold.

William said slowly, "I've come to some important conclusions lately. Been wanting to share them with you." He glanced at her finger. "Been thinking about the pearl or gold I once thought so important. I don't want them anymore. There are other pearls I'd rather have."

"What do you mean?" Julia couldn't help noticing how he seemed so at peace with himself.

"There are other pearls here in New Guinea. Remember the old chief and the witch doctor we went to see once?"

Julia nodded.

"I think they are pearls in God's kingdom. Their lives have been changed by God's love and forgiveness. I think now that *people* are beautiful pearls. And *you* are the most precious of all to me. But I won't press that point.

"There are pearls of beauty and grandeur in the hills and valleys of this country, majestic pearls most people will never see. There are pearls of wisdom in the Bible. There are pearls of sacrifice, like the missionaries make."

"Yes," Julie agreed, "I never thought about that."

"Not long ago, one night in a tent in a valley," William confessed, "I told God I wanted to be different. I settled it. God cleaned me up on the inside, and now I really want to live for him. I think he wants me to stay here—two years, ten years, or even a lifetime maybe—and use my talents for him. That's what I intend to do."

"Here? Maybe all your life?" Julia asked. "But . . . but it *rains* so much out here!"

William nodded slowly. "Yes, yes it does, Julie. But pearls are not harmed by water. They are *formed* in water!"

"But, William, that's quite a commitment!"

"Yes," he agreed quietly. "Someday, Julie, I hope you will make that same commitment to God, no matter where you're living."

Julia shook her head. She didn't feel like thinking about that. "Are you thinking about being a missionary?"

"No, but I've learned to appreciate missionaries since being out here. Always thought they were a strange breed before. But they come over here and work hard among these people as you know, teaching and preaching, setting up schools and clinics, building roads and power plants, and they do it for about half our salary. Marvin wants to marry Mary, but he won't ask her because he makes so little money."

"Mary would say yes. You know she would. Marvin probably knows it, too."

"He does, but he doesn't want to take what he feels is unfair advantage. When those missionaries started to build their power plant, several new workers came out from Australia to help them and at great personal sacrifice too. One fellow left his sheep farm in Australia because he also knew how to build dams. That was Mr. Oscar. One sold his machine shop and volunteered his services as a mechanic. That's Mr. Parry, who works with Marvin. Mr. Roper was nearly 60 when he came out as a carpenter."

"Why do they do it, William? What makes missionaries willing to make such a sacrifice and face such hard trials? I suppose it's that personal commitment you talked about."

"I know that's it. I've thought a lot about that, Red— "

The door opened and Mary and Marvin came in. "How do you feel, Julia? Like a cup of tea?" Mary took off her coat and Marvin hung it on a hook on the wall.

"I wouldn't mind. Will you have some, William?"

William nodded.

Soon Mary brought in the tea tray. *Mary looks happy*, Julia thought. "Marvin, we were just talking about missionaries when you and Mary came in. It's hard for me to understand why you do it, Marvin. What makes you stay here year after year working so hard and at such financial sacrifice? I can understand some of it. I appreciate helping a new country grow, but is that all of it with you? Is this going to be your life?"

Marvin, like William, was tall and lanky, but even thinner. He had hollows in his cheeks and his eyes were deep-set. His dark brown hair was thick, wavy and brushed back. His long fingers had signs of grease around the nails. He ran his fingers through his hair and answered slowly, as if sifting words, "Julia, I stay in New Guinea and work here because I must. I feel inside that I must be a part of doing God's work in this world."

"But it's not always fun to do what you *must* do," Julia interrupted.

"Oh, this is not an unwelcome 'must' or a 'must' based on guilt or fear. It's just because God loved me. So I must return my life in commitment to him."

"You feel you have to choose it?"

"Yes," he grinned, and the hollows in his cheeks deepened. "Yes, I choose it. But once I choose it, I have to make all my other decisions because of that choice. It's like a marriage vow. Once you take it, your other choices have to be in the light of that vow. I think a real Christian is joyful, fulfilled, enjoying the happiest life possible. He or she can walk free from guilt and fear. It doesn't mean Christians never have troubles or sorrows, they have plenty. But there is still joy inside because a Christian is in tune with God."

The tea warmed Julia as she struggled with these new ideas. Rain fell in noisy plops on the tin roof. "Tell me, Marvin, how did you come to make that commitment. How did you dare tie up your whole life like that?"

William and Mary sat quietly drinking their tea, listening to his conversation.

"I like to read the Bible, Julia. My reason comes from the first 11 chapters of Romans. There you find the love and mercy of God described. Then Romans 12:1 says, 'Present your bodies a living sacrifice, holy, acceptable unto God, which is your reasonable service.' That's what the Bible says, so I do it because I have faith in God."

"But I have faith in God, too, Marv!" Julia exclaimed. "Though I don't think I could do what you're doing. What do *you* mean by faith?"

Marvin hesitated, leaned back in his chair, thought deeply for a few minutes, then spoke sincerely. "It's hard for me to say it because I'm not a preacher. And the last thing I want to do is to sound like people who always tell you why they're so good! But *faith* in God means a lot more to me than just believing in God."

"What more?"

Marvin drank his tea. "We've hashed this out among ourselves over at the mission station. I can't say it as the bishop did, but I know it. Faith means first that I *accept what the Bible says about God*. That gives me security, something to put my feet down on."

"You mean something that keeps you steady," Julia observed.

"Yes. But faith also means that *I commit my life to my belief*. It means I do something to prove I believe it. Julia, have you ever seen those swinging bridges that New Guinea people weave out of vines and bamboo and hang onto a pylon on each side of a gorge?"

"Yes, I saw one when I was hiking with William. They scare me to death!"

"William, have you ever crossed from one mountain to another on one of those bridges?"

"Many times. Saves days of walking, but they scare me, too."

"Well, that's faith. You could believe forever that those bridges *would* hold you up and that's belief. But when you step out on one of those pitching, rolling, swaying bamboo bridges and go over a canyon, that's *commitment*. You believe so strongly it will hold you up that *you're committing your life to it*! That's faith. I felt God wanted me here. I'm here," he said simply.

"And I'm glad!" Mary interrupted.

Marvin smiled at her. "Still, faith is more, Mary." Marvin was now talking to Mary alone. Julia felt like an eavesdropper. Marvin continued, "Faith tells me God cares about *me*. I believe whatever happens in my life, he allows. If I'm in trouble, God gives me no explanation, but he's with me. That's enough. My faith in God helps me to understand my experiences in a way that makes sense. If I am happy, as I am with you, I believe God intends it."

Mary's eyes were bright with tears and she reached blindly for Marvin's hand.

Marvin clasped Mary's hand in his long fingers. "Another thing my faith does for me is that it gives me a big push to do this work which I feel called to do. Sometimes things seem hopeless, when all the motors stall within a few days of each other and parts are hard to get. But I remember I am a missionary, here to fix the mission cars, so other missionaries can do God's work too. When I am upset I read some promises in the Bible and know they are for me. Then I get the energy to go back to work."

Marvin paused for a long time, then nodded slowly, a look of decision on his face. "And, Mary, because of my faith in God, I've even got the courage to ask you to marry me—in front of William and Julia. You are the one I feel God wants for my good; he wants us together and I've loved you for a long time. I hope you feel God wants you to have me for *your* good. I've realized lately that, if I let you go back to Australia when your term is up, I would be missing the one he intended for me. Do you believe this?"

Mary hung on to his hand, tears of joy rolling down her cheeks. "I've known that for a long time, Marvin, but I thought you'd *never* get around to saying it!"

"If William and I had anywhere else to go," Julia croaked in her raspy voice, "we'd leave you two alone!"

Marvin smiled widely. "Don't worry, we've got the rest of our lives together. Just one more thing, Julia. I also believe in life after death, a life with Christ. I don't believe everything ends for me when I die. I think it's only the beginning of heaven."

The room was quiet. Marvin's long, thin hands held Mary's and their faces glowed. William sat with his legs stretched in front of him, nodding his head, thinking deeply. Julia sat with the flannel cloth around her throat, eucalyptus odors pervading the room. With his simple, profound words, Marvin had opened to her a whole new spiritual world. She had never been so moved before. She'd have to take some time to digest all this.

Finally William said, "Thank you, Marvin. I agree with everything you said. And it's changed my life."

Marvin pulled Mary to her feet, put his arm around her, and they walked out of the room without a word.

Julia broke the silence. "Marv is, like Mary said, a wonderful person. It must be a great feeling to know Jesus

Christ as well as Marv knows him. It would be nice to be that important to God."

William leaned over, put his hand gently on hers, kissed her on the forehead and assured her, "Don't worry, Red. You're important to God—and to me. Good night." He walked toward the door and bumped into a table on the way.

Chapter 9

"Julia, let's do something different tomorrow," Mary said as she came in the door one Friday afternoon. "There's a party going out to a mission station. Marvin, Mr. Roper and Mr. Parry are each driving a car. We'll drive about 25 miles out from here, but then we have to hike another 10 miles over the mountain to the station. Marvin says we can go if we want to. Are you game?"

"How about the office?"

"Grant will be away Monday anyway, and he has given permission for us to miss work. How about it?"

"Why are they all going?"

"The fellows are going to take a big load of supplies to the station hospital, and while there they will do some repairs and build a water tank. Marvin can bring us back Monday while the other men stay."

"Sounds like the last 10 miles will be a hard trek. But I'm game if you are. What do we have to take? We can't carry too much."

"We will have about 25 carriers anyway. Wear your hiking boots and slacks to keep leeches off your legs. Take your sleeping bag with your night clothes and carry your own water and sandwiches for lunch. We should be there by evening and we'll get supper there."

"Who lives out there?"

"A doctor and his wife, she's a doctor too, and two young women translators. The doctors are missionaries from the Cook Islands to New Guinea. They are nice; I met them once. They all live in a very primitive situation and don't even have a decent stove or water tank. So we will be roughing it! The materials have finally come, so Mr. Roper and Mr. Parry are anxious to go and build their water tank."

Julia had no idea how rough it would be!

They started off the next morning in three cars, each Land Rover pulling a trailer load of building and medical supplies. Twenty-five carriers from the doctor's village were to meet them at the place where they had to leave the cars. They had gone only five miles from home when the rain began. That was nothing new for the New Guinea highlands, of course, it just made the trip more difficult. Before the group got over the Bulai ridge, one of the cars had a flat. They had to partially unload that Rover to fix the tire, then reload. It took almost an hour in the rain.

With the Rovers in low gear and four-wheel-drive, they started up over a torturous mountain road. It could not be called a road—it was merely a wide trail. They bumped over rocks, through streams and around curves that hugged the cliffs. All the while rain continued. Julia wished she'd stayed at home and used the Saturday to wash her hair, mend clothes and read. But it was too late to think of that. Better to use the time now to do some praying that the Lord would help them get over that grim mountain.

Then they had to ford another stream, deeper than the previous ones had been. The first car got hopelessly bogged down. Everyone helped unload the car and trailer, hoping that when empty it could be moved. But even with all of them pushing, they still could not get the Rover out. By that time everyone was a bedraggled mess. There was no letup in the torrential rain and no native carriers to help. They just sat there, soaking wet. Julia wasn't a bit happy about the whole situation.

After about an hour a native appeared on the trail. Mr. Roper called to him, speaking in the indigenous language, and asked for help. The man began to sing out in a chant, loud and long. Soon other men in tanket leaves began to emerge from the forest, and within half an hour nearly 50 of them appeared.

They surrounded the mud-covered car, chanting, and literally lifted it, the trailer and the other two cars and trailers across the stream.

"Where did they all come from?" Julia asked.

"They all belong to one tribe that lives over on the other side of these woods. They call to each other in song like that, and one man passes the message along to another." Mr. Roper was unwrapping some small blocks of salt, a precious item to the New Guinea people. He offered each man a block in return for his help. The salt was quickly accepted.

Cars were reloaded and started again, the sturdy New Guineans following along for a time. The road was so poor and the going so slow that they had no trouble keeping up with the cars.

About noon they reached an appointed spot and met their carriers from the mission station, sitting under a rock ledge beside the trail, waiting.

Everyone piled stiffly out of the cars, joined the carriers under the shelter and ate lunch before setting out on foot.

As bad as the drive had been, hiking the last 10 miles was worse. From there on, it was up and over another mountain ridge. The villagers had unloaded their cars and trailers and equally divided equipment. They took the loads on their shoulders and started up through the jungle, the Bulai group following in single file. Mary went first, then Marvin, Julia, Mr. Roper and Mr. Parry, slogged through the wet, high grass. Fortunately the carriers ahead had shaken off most of the water from grass and trees as they passed. Sometimes someone stumbled over slippery stones and then was held up by another. Rain was beginning to let up a little, but still the walking was quite miserable.

Mary seemed happy—at least she was near Marvin. Julia found herself wishing she had broken her contract to the engineering company and gone back to Sydney with Graham. What an anachronism to be blundering over a forbidding mountain trail in New Guinea like this when she had the luxuries of Sydney waiting for her!

Well, no use thinking about that. Maybe a conversation, though difficult to carry on while climbing a mountain, would make the trek a little more interesting. Julia turned her head slightly. "Mr. Roper, how did you happen to come here? Were you just looking for a hard life?"

Mr. Roper smiled briefly. He was an older man, nearly 66, and had thick, bushy, gray eyebrows which jutted down at an angle and almost met above his nose. His hair, once black, was liberally sprinkled with gray, but his eyes were blue and kind.

He caught Julia as she stumbled on a stone. His Australian accent was broader than either William's or Marvin's. "You see, Miss Harrell, Oi'ma cahpenter, and Oi belonged to a group of people in mah church in Australia who had pledged to pray for mission work in New Guinea. We'd 'eard that the mission needed wohkers, so we began to pray that the Lo'd would send them. They needed four. We had been praying for four years. Oi didn't think Oi could come because Oi didn't have much education. But at prayer meeting one night, Oi looked down, and on the seat beside me was a paper telling about the need for wohkers in New Guinea. One thing they needed was cahpenters—not necessarily educated ones. Oi had no family and my circumstances at the time were such that Oi could come. Oi felt the Lo'd had this job just for me. Oi just had to come out 'ere."

"How long have you been here now?"

"Been 'ere six yeahs."

"Without a furlough? How could you stay so long?"

"As Oi said, Oi have no family, and there is so much wohk to be done 'ere. No one needed me in Australia, so Oi just stayed."

"Aren't you ever going back?"

"Prob'ly not. The Lo'd needs me 'ere to wohk for 'im."

Oh, the poor man, Julia thought, *living in a place like this for the rest of his life just because nobody needs him anywhere else!*

They crossed the ridge of this second mountain and straggled down the other side. This side was much more barren and rocky. The sea of kunai grass had stopped short of the summit, and without grass to hold the soil, much erosion was evident.

They could see the mission station in the distance. The spot for their compound with its small hospital, two homes and scattered out-buildings had been chosen with care. Behind the compound marched lines of tall casuarina trees, right up to the top of the mountain. But about 200 feet on either side of the mission compound, the soil was rutted where rain had washed down countless times. Today's rain was a muddy tumble in every direction. Off to the east, about half a mile from the mission was a village, also set in a grove of casuarina trees. Smoke hovered close over every low grass house scattered among the trees.

Darkness was upon them when the party reached the tiny mission station. Julia was so exhausted she could barely go the last half mile. As usual, going downhill had made her thigh muscles ache. What a relief just to sink on the mat-covered floor, pull off wet shoes and rub her legs!

Two young women translators from Melbourne were almost pathetically glad to see Mary and Julia. It had been several months since they had visited Bulai and had not spoken English to anyone other than themselves and the two doctors. They invited Julia and Mary to stay with them in their small house. The two from Bulai were grateful for the shelter, however primitive.

Their house was a simple one of four small rooms, with pit-pit grass walls, a corrugated-metal roof and woven mats over mud floors. They had built a quaint, brick stove in one corner of the kitchen, but there was no oven in the stove. Bread was baked in an iron pot over one of the open, round holes. They burned wood for fuel because it was readily available. Woodcutters brought loads every two weeks, they said.

The two girls, Gwen and Christine, were pretty and not much older than Mary and Julia. Julia could not help feeling sorry for them, buried so far in the wilderness, so far from all they'd ever known. But her pity was wasted. The two Melbourne girls took their situation in stride, so thoroughly were they absorbed in their work.

Mary and Julia gratefully accepted buckets of hot water for a bath. They unrolled their plastic-wrapped bundles and took out granny nightgowns, heavy socks and robes. The temperature had fallen with the heavy rains.

For supper they ate kau-kau, delicious when mashed with some canned butter. Rice, canned fish and hot tea appeared. What a welcome feast!

Gwen and Christine wanted to know all the news of the Bulai station. They announced with laughter that their radio had been out of order for several days, so they hadn't heard any news of the outside world. Only today they discovered that some rats had chewed through one of the wires. It was a simple matter to splice wires back together.

After supper the four sat near the brick stove to chat. It was the warmest place in the house. Julia was surprised at the amount of heat the stove put out into the room. They had no electricity; two gasoline lanterns supplied the light, though the flames flickered and hissed, and the lanterns had to be pumped up occasionally.

"Are there only four of you in this station?" Julia asked Gwen. "Don't you get terribly lonely?"

"Yes to both questions. The doctor and his wife are so

busy that we don't have much time together. Their fame is known all around, and they have so many cases that their little hospital is always full. They have only 10 beds though. Most patients prefer to come in for treatment and go back to their villages. About 500 people live in this nearest village. But cases come in from other villages, too."

"Where were these doctors trained?"

"They are natives of the Cook Islands, but they were trained in New Zealand. They're very dedicated people."

"They must be dedicated to stay here!" Julia exclaimed.

"They have a difficult case tonight, so things are tense over at the hospital. The chief of this nearby village has just brought in his young wife. She has been in labor for three days and the baby hasn't come. The doctor says the baby is dead, but the chief refuses to accept this and demands they bring a live baby. He's stirred quite a threat. A group of his relatives have been sitting outside the hospital door with bows, arrows and spears, watching to see what will happen. They will do anything the chief tells them to do."

Julia shuddered. "I wish I'd stayed in Bulai. Aren't you afraid?"

"No, not really," Gwen assured her. "The doctors have helped the chief and his family many times before, treating sores and malaria, worms, yaw and arrow wounds. And we have been teaching his wife to read and cook other things besides kau-kau. I don't think he will hurt anyone."

"Does the chief have any other children?"

"That's why he's so upset," Christine broke in. "He has three children, all girls. He has to have a son, he says. If this baby is a boy and dead, he will be furious and probably blame the doctor. He would never think of blaming himself for not bringing his wife in earlier. The baby might have been saved then."

"Are they going to operate?"

"They have to. Thank goodness, your party arrived with

the supplies! They were dangerously low on anesthetics and other drugs."

"Is the chief an old man?"

"No, he's a young man, I suppose about 25 or 30. He's strong, domineering, loud and proud, yet he's afraid, too. Like all the rest, he's afraid of evil spirits and magic. He is very fond of his wife—this is his second wife and she's only 16. Since he took her, he doesn't pay any attention to his first wife. Some people say, because of that, the first wife has worked malignant magic on the young wife and that's why her baby is dead."

Julia was only half listening to the last part of the conversation. She was too exhausted, and her eyes began to close in spite of herself. Yet even as sleep almost overcame her while sitting in the chair, the air seemed thick with a heavy sense of foreboding. She even thought the house was shaking, but she couldn't keep awake any longer. "Please excuse me," she apologized. "I have to go to sleep. That was the worst walk I ever took, and I'm dead!"

"So am I," echoed Mary.

"Just ignore the earth tremors," Christine commented. "We often have them here, but they never do any damage."

Julia and Mary unrolled their sleeping bags on narrow cots pushed against a drafty, pit-pit wall and were asleep almost before they could zip themselves in. But sleep was uneasy and throughout the night the cots quivered, and large raindrops clattered occasionally against the metal roof.

Julia awoke early the next morning to a brilliant sky, a dawn finger-painted with streaks of red and gold. Birds were raking up a quarrel outside the house, but everything else was still. The rain had stopped. She stretched her sore legs inside the bedding roll and groaned. There were stiff muscles where she didn't know she had muscles before!

Someone was tiptoeing around the kitchen and Julia smelled coffee. It made her realize how hungry she was. Her hiking clothes had been drying in the kitchen overnight, and she went out to dress by the fire.

Christine was there. She smiled, "Good morning. Did you sleep well?"

"I think so, but I heard it raining most of the night, and the earth kept shaking. I thought I was being rocked in a cradle part of the time. What's the news at the hospital? Did they get the baby?"

"Don't worry about being shook up a bit." Christine poured a cup of coffee for Julia. "We get quite a few earth tremors on this mountain but I haven't heard of any big quake. I suppose it *could* happen sometime. A few minutes ago one of the hospital helpers came over to bring some eggs. He said that at about midnight the operation was finished and the baby was a boy and was dead. The chief was so angry he didn't know what to do. He shook his spear at the doctor, who came out to tell him about the baby. But one of his relatives, an old man, said something which quieted him down."

"What did he say?"

"Something about, even if magic *had* caused the death of his baby, if the chief did anything to a good man like the doctor, then bad magic would punish him. Then Dr. Samson told the chief that his young wife was still very sick, but that the doctor and his wife would stay with her until she was out of danger. So the chief quit shaking his spear and shouting. He went over and sat by the corner of the house with his back to everybody. He is still there and looks so sorrowful. You can see him over there."

Christine pointed through a window. Across the yard Julie could see a group of brown men sitting under a tree, the rising sun glistening on their pig-fat-smeared bodies, their spears and arrows beside them. Some distance away, lonely in his grief, sat a solitary figure—brown, shining back bent over, red feather-crowned head bowed low. Even as Julia watched, a man she assumed to be Dr. Samson walked slowly out the door of the hospital and over to the chief. The proud warrior raised his head and looked up.

Dr. Samson put his hand on the chief's shoulder, talking earnestly to him. The girls could only imagine what was said, but action was instantaneous. Suddenly the chief leaped to his feet and with a terrible shriek, jabbed his spear toward the doctor. The doctor did not have time to sidestep, and the spear sank into his thigh. The chief threw back his head, yelling hatred toward the heavens. He was jumping and screaming the same word over and over. Then he suddenly whirled, jerked the spear from the doctor's leg and streaked out of the mission compound toward the village. Swift as lightning, his relatives with one motion were on their feet, spears in hand, shouting, rushing after their chief.

Julia realized her mouth was open and she was trying to cry out, but no sound came. The whole scene was like something from a horror movie. The doctor clutched his leg and fell. Julia found herself beside Christine, racing out the door toward him. Simultaneously they heard a muffled roar above the clamor of the men, and the earth shook violently beneath their feet. Both of them stumbled and fell. Julia realized this was more than just another small tremor. As they lay gasping, flat on the ground and nauseated with fear of the quaking earth, they looked up toward the shrieking chief and his relatives.

The mountain peak above them seemed to vibrate for a few seconds, to sink and disintegrate, then it thundered down upon the fleeing men, swallowing them completely. Mud and rocks, brown bodies, feathers and spears were tumbling toward the valley floor in a heaving, rolling mass.

Julia couldn't look anymore. Shuddering, she jammed her face in the dirt, covered her head with her arms and lay sobbing while the mountain roared down in front of her, rumbled beyond her and growled itself out in the valley below. Then stillness hung like the dawn of creation.

Gentle hands were helping her. "Are you 'urt, Miss Harrell?" Mr. Roper lifted her as he would a child. He seemed so strong. Marvin was helping Christine to her feet. Julia was crying hysterically, alternately pointing to the doctor on the ground and to the hillside where tragedy had taken place. Her words made no sense. Mr. Roper, talking gently, half dragged and half carried her like a limp rag doll back to the house. She was surprised to see the house still standing. Mr. Roper seemed so calm to have witnessed such horror.

"We often 'ave earth tremors 'ere in New Guinea, but this was the worst Oi've ever seen." He was looking around while talking soothingly to Julia. She gasped for breath and held on to him. "Looks like the hospital is still standing and the house 'ere," he said. "That casuarina forest above us saved the mission compound. And the village looks all right. But that unprotected area between this mission station and the village is totally covered. I doubt they'll ever find the chief and his men. Oh, it is very sad."

Julia looked back toward the village. No bright feathers anywhere between the mission compound and the village. Only mud and the stillness of death.

She looked again toward Dr. Samson. Two men had lifted him and were carrying him back inside the hospital. His wife in her white coat was walking beside him holding his hand.

Mary was standing in her long pink nightgown just inside the kitchen door. She was still vague with sleep. When she saw the four she cried, "Marvin, what—Julia, what *happened* to you? Christine! We must have had a bad earthquake. My bed shook so violently it woke me up. Oh, Julia, let me wash your face. You have dirt all over you! Did you fall down?"

Julia collapsed on her cot, so stunned she barely felt Mary washing her face and brushing off her clothes. When she awoke again it was noon and her face and body were bruised and aching.

It was impossible for her to go back to Bulai the next day, so Marvin radioed back the news. He thought Julia should rest for a few days before hiking back over the mountain.

When Christine and Julia could talk about what they had seen, they gradually gathered the rest of the story.

Dr. Samson had come out of his hospital to tell the chief that his young wife had just died. They had done everything they could. Christine and Julia had seen what happened next. The chief was so grief-stricken he went wild. In his first violent reaction he had jabbed his spear into Dr. Samson. Then he began shouting the name of his first wife and shrieking, "She put the magic that killed my man-child and my wife. I will kill her, I will kill her, I will kill her!" He had wrenched his spear from Dr. Samson's leg, whirled and ran. The two girls had seen it all.

That afternoon they watched sorrowing village man digging here and there in the slime, hoping to find the chief and their kinfolk. But the mud was thick and the gorge was deep. In despair they decided it was better to let them all remain in their burial ground.

No Australian had ever heard such wailing and groaning as then ascended from the village. It lasted for hours, until those mourning were too exhausted to lament anymore. Then they slept for a while and woke to wail again, their keening floating across the muddy waste.

Julia had seen death before. But she had never been near those who had no hope of life after death. The best they could hope for was that the spirits of those departed would not become malevolent; would not return for some revenge. Word filtered through that wives and daughters of the dead men smeared their faces and bodies with clay and chopped off finger joints in their grief. Julia grew ill with sorrow for their darkened minds.

News came to the mission that the first wife of the chief was living in terror for herself and her own children. She knew she had been blamed for "putting the Dewel" on the young wife and child which had brought on the second tragedy. She insisted she had nothing to do with it at all. Those left in the village council met and decided not to punish her. The spirits had caused the mountaintop to crumble upon the chief and his relatives while he was screaming for revenge. Perhaps it was because she was innocent. If so, no one could risk another catastrophe by touching her. If she were guilty, eventually her black magic would seek its own revenge.

For four days and nights Julia's mind was in turmoil. She was torn with grief and sorrow for the plight of those village people. They were so ignorant about God who loved them. They had no hope of any joy in this world or the next. Christine said that, on occasion, she had talked with the chief and his people about God and his love. She had told them the story of Christ on the cross. But to the villagers, he was just another man dying. How long would it take for them to believe! How long before they would have that life-changing experience! She wept for their ignorance.

On her narrow cot, when sleep would not come, Julia began to question her own life. *Do I really know anything about Jesus Christ? I have always considered myself a Christian—I have taught a Sunday school class. But I have never committed my life totally to Christ. If I had, would I still long for a life in Sydney society?* She finally fell asleep, not willing to probe anymore.

Mary, Marvin and Julia were planning to leave on the fifth day after the earthquake. The previous afternoon Julia was walking behind the tiny hospital among the casuarina trees. It was difficult to keep her gaze turned away from the devastated area between the mission compound and the village. Mournful cries still floated over the village. There was a great sorrow in Julia's heart.

Ambling up the slope through the casuarina grove, she saw someone come over the top of the ridge and start down toward her. William! Even at a distance she knew it was William and was not surprised at the joy she felt. She should have expected him. She walked faster to meet him, and when he saw her they both ran the last 50 yards. His arms were open and she ran into them. For a time they both forgot she was engaged to Graham.

"Oh, Julie! When I heard what had happened here, I came as fast as I could. Of course it took me all day!" He just stood and held her and she felt so safe with her head on his shoulder. "Are you all right?"

She looked up. "I'm all right, I guess, but I'm still bruised and sore. Christine and I were both thrown to the ground. Oh, William, I do appreciate your coming."

"I thought you might need me. Thank God, you are all right!"

She realized William was still holding her and she felt confused.

He lifted his head and listened to the sounds over the wasteland for a few minutes. "That's the women mourning in the village. How many were killed altogether?"

"I really don't know. There seemed to be between 10 or 15 in the group. Oh, William, it was an awful sight to see that mountain crumbling on top of those men! Come on into Christine and Gwen's house. They'll give you some supper. You must be tired."

His old grin was there. "Forgot all about being tired when I saw you, Red."

"We plan to go home tomorrow."

"I know. I'll just turn around and come with you. Have to get you safely back to Bulai."

That night Mary, Marvin, William and Julia sat around the brick stove with Gwen and Christine. Julia felt better with William near, but when a silence would fall into their conversation, sounds of the villagers' grief hung on the air.

Julia burst out, "I don't know how you can stand it, Christine and Gwen! You say you've been here five years working with these people. Yet it seems to me they are still caught as much in their old beliefs as they ever were."

Christine smiled. "No, not quite. If they had been, we'd all have been killed and maybe eaten too!"

"Well, why do you stay? Marvin has told us before why he does. But what motivates you?"

"It's very simple, Julia. We stay in order to show these people God's love. We want to learn their language so we can give them God's Word in their own language."

"How long do you suppose that will take?"

"We can show them love from the minute we arrive. All of us can show God's love if we have it in our own hearts. Then, depending on how fast we can learn their language, it will take perhaps 15 years to put one or two books of the Bible into their language. It usually takes that long to 'crack' a language, put an alphabet into writing, learn word meanings and idioms and then translate a gospel into that language."

"Do you really think it's worth it, Gwen? Seems to me that's the long way of doing things."

"It's worth it. When a native understands the Bible in his own language, he says to us, 'At last God has learned to talk in my language. Now I can truly understand what he means!'"

"Gwen, no doubt you and Christine are just the patient type to do this kind of thing. But it seems to me in terms of long-range planning, that is a poor way to teach them. I've been here listening to you and Christine study with your teacher, and I've come to some other conclusions."

"What are they?"

"I don't suppose you will agree with me," Julia said as she filled a coffee cup from the old-fashioned pot on the stove and passed it to William. "But once you put their language into writing, which you say takes 15 years, and you get a gospel from the Bible printed in it, then you still have to teach them to read. And once you teach them to read, the only thing they have to read is that one lone gospel! Now instead of *you* learning *their* language well enough to translate into it, why don't you learn it just well enough to be able to teach *them* English?

"That way, within the space of just one or two generations, you would have an English-speaking settlement. Then they would have the world of English books at their finger-tips to learn from. They could also learn about cleanliness which they so badly need, how to prevent disease, how to cook and care for their families. They could learn history, geography, everything would be available to enrich their lives. By doing it your way, they are shut up in one small por-tion of literature. It doesn't seem to me to be the best way." Julia stopped, out of breath.

"But wouldn't you rather be able to read the Bible in your own mother tongue," Gwen asked, "than having to try to un-derstand it in a foreign tongue?"

Julia nodded. "No doubt I would. But, I've thought a lot about this since coming here. Even if I would rather read in my own language, does that warrant all the expense and waste of man-hours—even years—to put the gospel into my lan-guage if just a few hundred or even a few thousand people use it? If you would use the same money to establish English schools in every village, within the same 15 years you would have a new generation of English-speaking children. And I've heard it is easier for a second generation to learn Eng-lish. Then your school could be there to give them a higher degree of education in all the books available to them in Eng-lish. I'm not at all downgrading the value of reading the Bible. I'm saying, though, to be able to read only the Bible is not educating them enough to live. Their lives will not be advanced economically. Goodness, what a speech that was!"

William smiled at her, but he just sat, drank his coffee and listened.

Christine argued, "But they need to be converted from pa-ganism. English education could never produce that. As they are, these people are fear-ridden, cruel and repressive. But the Christian doctrine is rich in love, grace and mercy. Even if they had nothing else, to me it would be worth my life. One New Guinean said to me, 'Reading God's talk in another lan-guage is like eating strange food; you eat and eat but your hunger still dances. Reading God's talk in *my* language is like eating sweet potatoes from my own garden. At once my full stomach dances and I am satisfied."

William spoke out, "Christine, I feel humble when I see your dedication to God in doing this kind of work. On the other hand, Julia, you have some strong arguments, and I too believe in a broad education for all New Guinea people. There's one thing to think about, though. It seems a pity for any culture to be completely lost. The fact that Christine and Gwen and others in their occupation perpetuate this native language—this would go far to prevent ethnic suicide, wouldn't it?"

"Everyone is proud of his own language and customs," Marvin spoke. "When he sees that other people are interested enough in him to spend a lifetime learning his language and ways, it must influence him to listen to that person explain a better way of believing. Isn't that true?"

Gwen nodded, "Absolutely! To speak to a man in his own language is the only way to reach him. Then the gospel can become a part of his own culture, rather than a superficial borrowing. Only when a man has the gospel in his own *thinking* language will he be able to ponder on it and accept its truth. *We* say it is 'the bread of life' because bread is our basic food. But to them the Bible becomes the 'sweet potato of life' because that is *their* basic food. They call it 'the delicious story.' That's one important reason for translating the Bible into *their* language. You have to use their idioms."

"And what if you fail?" Julia asked. "What if, after you've worked years teaching them, they still do not believe in God, and cling to their old evil ways? Then they have neither a better moral life nor an education."

Gwen pondered awhile; then, "I would be disappointed, of course. I'm human and like to succeed. But I have to remember that God never called me to be successful. All He requires is that I be *faithful*. Success is a by-product. I have to leave the results to him after I've done my best."

Julia was thoughtful. "I had never considered," she admitted, "that perhaps God never called us to be successful. I thought success should be everybody's goal."

"I'm puzzled," Mary commented. "I wonder why God wouldn't want us all to be able to communicate by having a universal language? Looks as if that would have made your task as missionaries so much easier. But, there's the Tower of Babel."

"I don't see how we could know God's mind as to the reason," Marvin spoke slowly. "But won't it be magnificent on the great resurrection day when every redeemed man is praising God in his own language?"

"It could be," Christine suggested, "that one language could never be adequate, with its own peculiarities and limitations. Each language has its own beauty of idiom and phrasing, lilt and cadences of sound, and it probably will take them all together to do a proper job of glorifying God, as it says in Revelation that we *will* do."

No one could think of anything to add to that. Finally Julia said, "Well, it's a deep subject and I don't know all the answers. But I'm beginning to learn. I've learned a lot here too, Gwen and Christine. Thank you."

Mary stood up. "I'm sleepy. And if we are going to hike 10 miles tomorrow, we'd better get some sleep. Gwen, Christine, I appreciate both of you so much, for all your hospitality and kindness and inspiration."

"So do I," Julia echoed. "And I'm humbled when I see your dedication to God's work. It's something I haven't had because I'm simply too materialistic. No doubt the world is much better for having people like you in it. How do they say it here? 'I'm putting my stomach for you!' Someday, I might even be convinced you're right."

Chapter 10

*T*heir trek back over the mountain was uneventful and tiresome, but with William along, it seemed much easier. Once Julia had thought Bulai was primitive with its holes-in-the-bucket shower, but it seemed like a corner of paradise in comparison to the out-station hospital compound.

William came by the office a few days later and sat down by Julia's desk. "Are you feeling all right now, Julie?"

"Oh, yes, I'm okay. I was thankful for Mr. Roper the day the earthquake struck. He was so kind and gentle. William, just to look at him, one would not realize his calm competence in the face of tragedy. He must have been literally as shaken as I was, yet his concern was for me and the way I felt. I have a great appreciation for him."

"Did I ever tell you about his run-in with the Bulai chief who nearly killed him?"

"No. You mean the same chief who got so angry when Megia was baptized?"

"The same one."

"I'd like to hear about it."

William began to mimic Mr. Roper's way of speaking. "*Oi'm a cahpenter and Oi'm a Christian*—"

Julia had to laugh. William sounded just like him.

"Don't laugh, Red. He's a great guy. He told me all about his clash with the chief—

"The bishop had instructions from the power-line builders that two trees were in the path, and the trees would have to go. So the bishop told Mr. Roper to go up and fell those trees. Now these New Guinea people love their trees, and they are also fearful of the spirits in them. So they didn't want him to cut any down. You see, over in this country, the mission cannot own any land; they can only lease it. That's the same way with all of us; only New Guinea people can own land.

"Well, Roper started off on his job of cutting the trees, but the big chief of this territory went wild. Roper didn't know at first he *was* the chief when he came at Roper shaking his spear. He demanded that Roper pay for the trees; five Australian dollars for each. Roper didn't understand much of the chief's language then, but he said he understood *that*!

"He always reads his Bible before daylight, and the next day he read from the Sermon on the Mount: 'Love your enemies . . . do good to them that hate you.' He had no idea how much those words would be needed that day.

"That afternoon when he felled one tree, some of the native boys standing around, probably spying, sang out over the hill in their chant. Soon that old chief roared up over the hill, wild with rage. He was actually hurling dirt in the air, and even throwing some in his mouth just to show his anger. He had a huge knife in his hand. He bent over and cut a big limb off the felled tree and came toward Roper with it. Roper said he remembered that just a few years before the chief had been a cannibal. Roper reached down and got his axe and threw it down the mountain out of the chief's reach. Roper was not armed with anything—he said the Lord wouldn't let him pick up anything against the old chief."

"Do you think the chief really intended to kill Mr. Roper?"

William nodded. "Probably, just to teach the white people a lesson. The chief began to hit him with the big limb—he bears the scars to this day. Now that morning when he left for work, Roper had put a five-pound note into his shirt pocket. He intended to pay the chief what he had demanded for one tree. When the chief began to hit him with the limb, that five-pound note fell out of his shirt pocket and landed on the ground at the chief's feet. The chief reached down and picked it up, his anger a little less, but he was still snarling.

"All the time he was hitting Roper, he—Roper—was backing up closer to the top of the hill. All the rest of their men were working over on the other side of the hill and didn't know what was going on.

"Just after the chief got the money, Roper backed up over the top and met the rest of the group. The chief wouldn't dare tackle the whole bunch, so he went off down the mountain, raging all the way. Roper had taken a hard beating, but he said he couldn't hate the chief. The Lord had told him just that morning through the Bible verse, to love his enemies, and he did. Today the chief is like a brother to him. Roper says, 'Of course the chief isn't a Christian, but 'e's my friend. Perhaps 'e will be a Christian someday.'

"And perhaps he will," William added, "but he was angry all over again when Megia became a Christian! He hasn't tried to do anything about it though. Megia is not a bit afraid of him."

When William finished with Mr. Roper's story, Julia was in tears. "That quiet little fellow has been through all that? He looks so . . . so insignificant. He doesn't dress neatly and his hands are permanently grimed. I'm sure he can't get them clean. He's shy and doesn't talk much."

"That's right," William agreed. "I had to pull that story out of him. And you know, he's been here six years and hasn't even told anybody when his birthday is. He doesn't want anyone making a fuss over him."

"We ought to select a day and say it's his birthday and make a cake and special dinner for him anyway! Maybe Mary and I can do it sometime."

William took a deep breath. "Julie, your time here in Bulai is short, and I don't see much of you anymore. Come over for dinner tonight and cheer up a lonesome bachelor?"

Julia nodded. "After last week, I need a lonesome bachelor to talk to. What time?"

"I'll come for you about seven o'clock."

When they arrived at William's house that evening, Sekiba was actually singing in the kitchen, if one could call his kind of three-toned chant "singing." He seemed bursting with joy. He fairly pranced into the room when he served pineapple juice.

"You seem mighty pleased with yourself for some reason today, Sekiba," William remarked. "What's the occasion?"

Sekiba grinned widely. "Yessum, Mastah, me very pleased. Megia get wide hips now—gonna get baby! Sekiba got'im pine wife. Raise lotsa pigs too!"

William and Julia both laughed. "Congratulations on both the baby and the pigs!" Julia raised her glass to him.

Sekiba stood indecisively for a few moments. "Mastah?"

"Yes?"

"You gonna go 'long let pink-misis marry with 'nother fella?"

William didn't look at Julia. "She chose him, Sekiba. He's a nice fellow."

"You ought'ta go 'long marry pink-misis, Mastah. You laik 'em want 'em her?"

"Wish I could marry her, Sekiba." William looked straight at Julia. "She knows I want her."

Julia felt as if she were a piece of furniture under discussion.

"Maybe if Mastah rich man, pink-misis marry Mastah." He raised his eyebrows and grinned in Julia's direction.

William shook his head. "Not just for money, she wouldn't."

Sekiba started slowly out of the room, then hesitated and looked back. Shrugging his shoulders, "Ah don'no, Mastah, she too much little. Maybe hard time with baby."

Julia gasped.

"I'd take her anyway," William laughed. "Serve the dinner, Sekiba. Let's not let her starve to death!"

Julia had only one more month until her term of service was up. One Saturday she and Mary packed a lunch, William and Marvin came by in a Land Rover, and the four started off for a picnic. It was a beautiful morning, bright and warm. They bumped over rocky roads until they came to a narrow path of a road winding up a tree-covered slope. "Hope we don't meet anybody on this road!" Julia said. "This is nerve-racking."

"Stick with me, Red," William advised. "I'll take care of you."

In the jolting back seat, Mary said dreamily, "Go anywhere you want to, William; Marvin's going to take care of me."

Everybody laughed.

William parked the Rover near a large tree which slanted out over the hill. Julia jumped down from the car and stood looking over the mountains, ridge after ridge. "Look at that scene! This is what I'm going to miss, these gorgeous views." She was instantly sorry she'd said it. A bleak look flashed across William's face as he turned away.

"Let's eat," Mary suggested hurriedly. She, too, had seen William's face.

While they were eating, sitting on the slope under the tree, they gazed down. "Where does that little path go?" Julia asked. "Looks like it winds in and out of the jungle of trees all the way down to the valley."

"It does," William replied. "I've trekked it more than once. It goes to a village at the bottom. In that village live some families who carve shells, particularly beautiful 'name shells.'"

"Why are they called 'name shells'?"

"Because they are carved into a certain design, and the

carver 'names' them. They are much more expensive than ordinary shell necklaces."

"You mean they live way down there and have to climb all the way up here to get on the road to Bulai?"

"Yes. They've hidden their village for protection from their enemies. Want to go see?"

Everyone agreed they should. So after eating, they set off at a leisurely pace; William in the lead, then Mary, Marvin and Julia brought up the rear. "Stick with us, Red," William reminded. "The path is narrow, and steep in some places."

They trekked down the path just wide enough to go single file, the men turning often to help Mary and Julia over particularly difficult spots. Tree ferns drooped from above and had to be brushed from their faces. Overhead trees sometimes arched thickly together, almost creating a state of twilight at noon. Sometimes growth alongside obscured the path, and only three heads bobbing up and down ahead gave Julia directions. The path was beaten hard as if thousands of bare feet had trodden here. No doubt they had. Sometimes another path crisscrossed theirs, wandering off in another direction, and sometimes their path was not hindered by trees at all. It was still and warm, for here and there the sun's rays filtered through even the thick green canopy.

Julia ambled along, dreaming about Graham. Sometimes she'd almost forgotten how he looked, but today his image was clear in her mind. He was so handsome—Mrs. Graham Moresby! Mrs. Graham—

A sound startled her and she whirled around. There, just over her head, was the most gorgeous bird she'd ever seen—brilliant greens and blues, with yellow edged in black on the side of its head. Its tail was long, green and feathery, curling and swaying in the breeze. "A bird of paradise!" she whispered to Marvin, but he was too far ahead to hear her. She stood still to watch the bird for a moment, wishing she could catch it. She knew that few people were ever privileged to see a bird of paradise in the forest. What a beautiful going-away present, a glimpse of one of the wonders of New Guinea. Then the bird's tail waved as it lifted from the branch and disappeared into the dark green overhead. Julia sighed, turned and plodded on, trying to catch up with the others, but at that moment her toe caught in a tree root, and she fell sprawling.

"Ooooo—" her breath was almost knocked out of her. She lay gasping for a moment, got up and brushed off her knees. Walking faster than before she called, "Marvin," but her breath came in a hoarse squawk. Never mind, she'd catch them.

Ignoring her throbbing knee, she plunged faster into the green thicket. "Marvin, Mary, William!" How could they be so far ahead? She walked faster, head down to see the path.

It took her about five minutes more to realize she'd taken the wrong way. *I must have taken another path at right angles to our path after watching the bird. When I whirled around to see it, I guess I became confused in my directions. What an idiot to drop so far behind the others, but I'd been thinking about Graham!* She turned around again and began to retrace her steps, looking for the intersection to the path.

"William, Mary, Marvin!" she shouted. But only thick, silent green engulfed her. Sound could not carry very far through it. She must have reached the point where the path crossed the right one, but there was no sign of it! *Face it, Stupid, you're lost in a jungle. Now don't panic!*

What should she do? Keep on going and try to catch up, or sit still and wait for them to miss her and come back? She felt like an utter fool. Getting lost was the kind of thing a child would do! *I must be accident-prone or something!* Perhaps the best thing to do now was to do nothing.

Having decided that, she sat down on the ground in the middle of the path. *If anybody comes this way, they'll have to walk right over me!* She waited and waited. She must have been sitting there for an hour. Her leg ached and she was frightened. What if they couldn't find her? *What if someone* who's never seen a white woman comes along, such as, perhaps, a young, fierce chief with a big spear and no mercy? The only sound was an occasional shriek of a parrot.

These people used to be cannibals. It is silly to think about that, for they are different now. But suppose they still are? What if they are still cannibals in secret? Nobody would ever know what happened to me!

Her knee was swelling and she rubbed it to relieve the pain. She thought she heard William calling, "Julia," but it was only a bright red parrot flashing by. *What am I doing in New Guinea anyway? I ought to be in Graham's house in Sydney, wearing silk and driving a big car and being cared for. Any woman is crazy who would find herself lost on a wild New Guinea mountain with only savages and parrots around.* She was thirsty, too.

The sun was making her sleepy. *If I go to sleep, maybe I will never wake up. Maybe a native will spear me while I'm sleeping. Goodbye, William. I'm sorry you didn't find me in time.* Her head dropped and she dozed, snapped upright at a noise and dozed again. Then she slept, though for how long, she didn't know. Suddenly William was there, shaking her and calling back over his shoulder to Mary and Marvin, "Here she is!"

Through bleary eyes, she saw Mary and Marvin peering around William's shoulder. Then they turned and sat down.

"Wake up, Julia. Are you all right? Thank God, you are! I was so worried. We couldn't find you. How'd you get way over here? You're a quarter mile off the path!" William pulled her to her feet, enfolded her in his arms and she stood trembling, her head on his shoulder.

Julia's tears were tears of pain and relief. "Oh, William, I'm sorry. For the second time in two weeks I've been scared to death. I was an idiot to stop, but I saw a bird of paradise and stopped for only a minute. Then I took the wrong path and fell down and my knee hurts." She realized she sounded like a lonely little girl.

"Never mind." She felt amazingly protected in William's arms. "When you don't stick with me, Red, you always get into trouble, don't you?"

Julia sniffed. "Looks like I always do."

William was shaken. "We'll go home and visit the shell village another time if we can. It'll soon be dark up here." With his arms around her she limped back up toward the car. Before reaching it, a gray curtain of rain swept across the mountain, obliterating the green valley.

Chapter 11

*I*t was almost time for Julia to leave Bulai and she began to sort her belongings, giving Megia and Mary things she didn't want to take. As Mrs. Graham Moresby, there would be plenty of new clothes and household linens. While she was packing one day, William knocked.

"Hi, Red. I've just had a great idea. Actually, I have to be honest and say I had the idea a long time ago. That's why I extended my term of service by a few months."

"I *thought* you were staying longer than you needed to this term."

"Not longer than I *needed* to; I *needed* to be near you. You're always getting into trouble when I'm not there." He grinned. "Anyway, I have a great idea. I want to go to Australia with you and the big Mount Hagen sing-sing festival is on just when you are supposed to leave here. Will you come with me to Mount Hagen and see it before going on to Sydney? It's the best show ever in New Guinea, and there's nothing like it anywhere else in the world. You really should see it before leaving for good."

"What's it like?"

"It's an annual affair. Warriors from all over this area of New Guinea will be there, dressed in all their battle regalia, and they compete in singing and dancing. If you will go with me, I will fly on to Sydney with you. We can stay with some friends of mine in Mount Hagen."

"Sounds like a great idea! I've heard of this great sing-sing and I'd love to see it. Reserve a place for me with your friends."

"Sekiba has asked for permission to come along with us. As a child he used to dance in the sing-sing competitions, and he wants to see this one."

"Megia isn't planning to go, is she?"

"No, not with a baby coming. She'd better stay here."

So Julia was spared the pain of saying good-bye to William in Bulai. The day of their departure dawned sharp and clear. The little plane was waiting on the airstrip when Mary took her over in the company car. William and Sekiba were already there.

It was hard to say goodbye to Mary. She had been very quiet for the past week. "I wish I could come to your wedding, Julia." Mary wiped her eyes.

"So do I. In fact, I don't see how I can get married without you. I wish I could stay here for yours."

Mary hugged her again. "It's only one month away, as soon as Marvin gets back from this trip to another mission station. Oh, Julia, I'm so happy. Marvin's the most wonderful person I've ever met in my life." She looked a little uncomfortable then pulled Julia aside from the others. "Can I say something to you? I've been debating it for a week."

"Of course."

"Julia, you can tell me to mind my own business, and I'd deserve it. But I have to say this; it's my last chance. The man you are marrying must really be great for you to turn William down. I think William is absolutely first-class. I really wish you were marrying him because I think you two are just made for each other. And he is so much in love with you!"

Julia was touched. "I know, Mary. William is a wonderful person, but I'm in love with Graham."

"Don't make a mistake about this, Julia. Please be sure.

Remember what we were talking about once when you first came, about how somebody said that God had the best person picked out for each one of us to marry? And if we missed his choice for us, then we would never be as happy?"

"I remember."

"Well, just be *sure* that Graham is the one God has chosen for you. It's your whole life, Julia!"

"I know."

"Well, whoever gets William is going to be lucky. I don't know what he will do here without you." Mary kissed her. "Goodbye, Julia. God bless."

Grant Richards drove up to see them off. He shook Julia's hand with a strong grip. "Goodbye, Julia. Thank you for being such an efficient secretary. I doubt if Banner will be any good when he returns without you, though. All the best! Tell Moresby he's getting a gem. And if Sydney doesn't suit you, please come back. It will take me quite a while to find someone as efficient as you."

Sekiba climbed into the plane with them and they all strapped down their seat belts. The little plane scooted down the runway, its passengers waving to Mary, Grant and Megia who were standing there waving back.

Julia had not expected to feel quite so sad when she left Bulai. After all, she was going home to be married. But she did feel sad, and pressed her face against the window so William would not see her tears. Probably she would never see Bulai again.

William was fortunate to have friends in Mount Hagen who put them up, because the town was overflowing with thousands of visitors from all over the country. Every room in every hotel was booked, and many slept out in the open, in small tents or under the trees. William, Sekiba and Julia pushed their way through the crowded streets. New Guinea people were there from many tribes and clans, each dressed in his own fashion of feathers and wearing his best pearl shells. Julia saw one man wearing what appeared to be a saucer strapped to his forehead. "Look, William, why would that man want to wear a saucer on his head?"

William pretended to look amazed at her ignorance. "Why, don't you know that a saucer on the forehead is the latest style? Once a friend of mine who lives here in Mount Hagen said that a saucer is the one dish which is most often stolen from any kitchen. They drill two holes in it so they can tie it up like that. It's the next best thing to a pearl shell."

Julia laughed. "And look there, William," she whispered, "at this man next to me. He has a toothbrush tied to his arm. Do you think he wears it just so he won't lose it? Do you suppose he uses it?"

Just then the man grinned, showing strong, red, betel-nut-stained teeth that had never known a brushing.

"No," William declared. "The function of a toothbrush means nothing to that fellow. He happens to like the pretty green plastic handle, so he wears it simply as a decoration." He looked closely at her. "Julie, may I advise you on something?"

"Of course."

"Well, I think it would be a good idea if you took the pearl off your finger. There are too many people here, and nobody can miss seeing that pearl! It is tempting to many, and someone may steal it."

"Do you think so?"

Sekiba broke in. "Yes, Misis. Pearl may get 'em stolen. It very big. People like 'em pearl!"

"Yes," William continued. "Put it in your purse or on a chain around your neck. Better not take a chance."

"Okay, if you think that's best. I have a small chain here in my purse with another pendant on it. I'll use that." So Julia put the ring on the chain and hung it inside her dress so the pearl was not visible.

The sing-sing competition had grown out of the New Guineans' love for their village sing-sings. Thousands of eager participants looked forward each year to coming to

Mount Hagen or Goroka. Each town took it in turn. Smaller villages held their own shows, but these main festivities attracted the greatest crowds. Every adult person in each village had practiced long hours for this.

William, Sekiba and Julia managed to sit under a tree, squeezed in with hundreds of people, mostly well-greased, decorated natives. It was impossible to move. The odor was nauseous. People wore rows and rows of beads and huge shells around their necks, net bags (billums) slung from the women's heads, and all wore bark bracelets around their arms. Their faces were decorated with white, black, yellow, red, blue and green paint, with grotesque eyes and noses painted on. Sometimes elongated noses were marked with white, edged in black. Some men had large pigs' tusks stuck through their noses and enlarged ear lobes, and some had bird of paradise feathers through pierced septums. All men wore high headgear made of tall feathers or human-hair wigs. Bones of large cassowary birds were also used as decorations. Varicolored grass skirts swayed on vibrating hips.

The sing-sing started, and as stars spangled a velvet sky, everyone was transported back into a wild past. The dancing was almost overpowering in its masculinity, with long lines of half-bare, plumed dancers surging, stamping, advancing, retreating. Weird chants droned above the ground rumble of flat-footed stamping. Faces were fierce with concentration and glowing paint. About half the men danced with small, black *kundu* drums, their thick hands crashing down in rhythm on the snakeskin drumheads. Others danced with long spears and bows. The mass of surging participants spread out in front of the onlookers like a great sea of undulating plumes, or a wild army of tossing feathers.

Sometimes above the drum thunder one could hear a faint tinkling like thousands of bells. This sound came from *tambunam*, the sea-snail shells—shining iridescent—which each man wore in ropes tied to his waist. Every movement of his body caused them to jingle. The sound was like Christmas bells in a rumbling thunderstorm.

The drums boomed in a constant rhythm—softer and louder, farther and nearer, like a rolling surf inundating a quiet shore. It almost hypnotized Julia, then unnerved her to be in the middle of such spectacular power.

Sekiba sat entranced.

Julia sat as long as she could keep awake. Finally she said, "Let's go, William. I'm about to fall asleep on your shoulder, and this will go on all night."

"That sleeping on my shoulder sounds good," William remarked. "Let me enjoy being with you now before I get that king-sized heartache when I see you with Moresby."

As they walked to William's friends' home, he said, "Tomorrow is your last day in New Guinea. I've planned something different for us, and I hope you will enjoy it. I've hired a car and we'll go down to the bird of paradise sanctuary. It's about 40 miles I think. I've been told it is a beautiful spot, and I'd like to see it with you before you leave. The birds live in huge cages in their natural habitat. You'll see a few animals there too. Sekiba saw it once, he says."

William and Julia walked downtown the next morning, pushing their way through throngs of village people. Mount Hagen was a nice town with new buildings going up, paved roads and a good-sized shopping area featuring goods from all over the world. They hired a small car and drove leisurely for an hour and a half. The road was extremely dusty and bumpy, but the views on hilltops were spectacular. Green, fertile valleys and purple mountains in the distance. Gentle slopes and rocky, razor-backed ridges. They stopped several times to take pictures.

When they arrived at the sanctuary, they washed the dust off their hands and faces in a stream which meandered through the soft green. They decided to make a tour before eating the picnic lunch their friends had given them. As they had heard, birds of all kinds and a few small animals were housed in giant bamboo cages. Large trees grew inside the cages and jungle surrounded them.

"Look, William. That sign says that little animal is a tree kangaroo, but he looks like a baby bear. Look at his pink nose."

"He does look like a baby bear until you see his long, strong tail."

"He doesn't seem to have much pep today."

"He's a night prowler. In the daytime he's droopy like a man with a hangover."

By far the most spectacular birds were the birds of paradise, for which the sanctuary was named. All the other birds were dull by comparison.

"William, I didn't realize there were so many species of the bird of paradise. Look at all the different ones," Julia read them off: "King of Saxony, look, we saw some long streamers like those in the bird's tail through some noses last night!"

"Yes, we did."

"Princess Stephanie, Ribbon-tail Bird of Paradise, The Sicklebills, The Lesser Bird of Paradise, Raggaina, The Red-plumed . . . William! This is the kind I saw in the jungle that day when I got lost! Isn't he beautiful? Look at the yellow and black on his head! Uh, I'm not sure, though. I remember that one had a long, plumy tail. They are all so beautiful!"

"I've heard," William remarked, "that the female bird of paradise lays only one egg at a time because that is all she can feed. The male is a natural philanderer and a poor husband. While she's feeding her young, he's off shaking his feathers in a love dance for another female."

"Some bird! All beauty and no morals."

William and Julia ambled from one cage to another, down narrow paths. William took a bamboo flute from his jacket pocket and tried to imitate some of the birdcalls.

Though he came close to imitating their calls, the birds would not respond. So he gave up trying to be a bird and surprised Julia by swinging into "Waltzing Matilda" on the flute.

"I didn't know you could do that!" she exclaimed. "Why haven't you played for me before?"

"Part of my fatal charm is to keep the girls ignorant of some of my talents!" He grinned. "Yet my repertoire is limited. I hope you really appreciate it because, if we were Bulai people, you would never be allowed to hear me play my bamboo flute."

"Really? Why not?"

"Well, for some reason when a Bulai man wants to play a flute he goes off by himself into the woods and no woman is ever supposed to hear him. It's bad luck, I guess."

"Could be he's such a poor musician that he knows she couldn't stand to listen!"

"For that remark you have to sing a solo."

So he played "Waltzing Matilda" again, and Julia sang as they strolled through the sanctuary, lingering to look at the birds and enjoying each other's company. She felt so at home with William. They were alone in a seemingly vast wilderness; they had met no one at all in the sanctuary and the only sound was an occasional birdcall.

A sudden thought jarred her: *Enjoy William's company now! This is the last time you'll ever be with him like this.* Her next thought was, *I can't stand that. Never see William again?* She turned her face away, lest he read what was written there. "Oh, look, William! Here are the cassowaries! Aren't they huge, and aren't they an ugly gray! No pretty feathers at all! Don't they belong to the emu family?"

"Perhaps, but they are a little smaller. These cassowaries are about five feet tall; emus are about six, so they tell me."

"Look, they have only three toes and no pretty tails like peacocks, or plumes like birds of paradise. Why do the New Guinean people think they are so great? Why do they love these big old birds?"

"Oh, to care about birds may not be so unique, Julie. In Greek mythology a connection was made between birds and divine spirits. And in Siberia, *shamans* (medicine men) sometimes imitate bird sounds in their religious rituals."

Julia was surprised. "Now how would you know that? You're brilliant!"

William looked pleased with the compliment but he shrugged, "Oh, this old professor likes to read and study Greek mythology sometimes as a sort of hobby. And I'm interested in anthropology too."

"Well, I am impressed, Mr. Banner! I've heard that cassowary eggs are very strong and smell awful."

"The eggs are, and they do. One egg will make an omelet for a whole family, but I don't like their taste at all. I think owning a cassowary is more of a status symbol than anything else. Like carrying an airline bag. You know how an almost naked villager will carry an airline bag and an umbrella if he can get one!"

"You're so smart. How'd you ever get so much information, and you so young too!" She giggled. "I saw another real status symbol the other day. A stark-naked little boy with a runny nose was walking proudly down the middle of the road blowing bubble gum all over his face!"

She laughed and strolled away from the cassowary cages. The laugh seemed forced to her own ears, and she wondered if William noticed. She knew he was deliberately trying to forget that it was their last day together; it was in his eyes every time he looked at her. Why did life have to get so mixed up and difficult? Could she be in love with two men at the same time? *Oh, William, why are you so dear to me when I'm in love with Graham?*

While William was fooling with his camera, trying to get it focused on a cassowary bird still near the fence, Julia sauntered on down the path, savoring the lush, green beauty and stillness. It was like the Garden of Eden. The path wound steeply down from the cassowary cages, snaking through a natural rain forest. This was the densest part of the sanctuary. On each side of the path, bamboo clumps grew tall and thick, their plumes twined about by roots and drooping exotic flowers. Parasitic plants of all kinds grew high on many trees, waving feathery plumes and increasing foliage density. She could not see the sky here; overhead was only arching, towering green. Orchids were abundant.

Just a curve in the path out of William's sight but still within hearing distance, she called back, "Come on, William, you can't afford any casso—" And then it happened! Suddenly, without a sound, a thick, strong arm smeared with pungent pig grease clamped around Julia's mouth and face, cruelly cutting her cheek with its harsh, bark bracelet. She tried to scream, but could only grunt. She looked mutely and swiftly up into a horribly painted warrior's face—red-and-white-gashed cheeks, two huge pigs' tusks stuck through the nose and turned up (the way they used to wear them during a battle) and a mass of tall, white feathers on his head.

When she tried to open her mouth to scream, the arm was jammed tighter, cutting off all sound. The warrior's hand lunged down her neckline, grasped the pearl ring and with a jerk broke the chain, painfully cutting her neck as he did so. Then she was released and pushed to the ground. It had only taken a few seconds. Without a sound the warrior faded into thick jungle growth.

Julia lay there for a few moments, stunned and quivering, catching her breath with great, gasping sobs. "William, oh, William!" she tried to cry out, but little sound came from her aching throat. William was there almost immediately, a look of incredulity on his face as he tenderly lifted her. "Julie! Red! What in the world! What happened to you!"

"The ring! My pearl is gone!" She fell against him with hysterical sobs and he held her close.

"Stop shaking, my darling. It's all right. I'm here. I've got you," he soothed her, not seeming to be aware of what he was saying. "Oh, Red, I always let you get into trouble when you leave me! How could I ever let you out of my sight!"

He carried her easily. The world spun around and she

clung to him. He carried her down the hill and put her in the picnic shelter, wet his handkerchief in the stream, and gently washed her injured cheek and neck. Julia was still gasping and shaking.

"Now," he ordered, "tell me what happened."

"I was only a few steps away from you," she squeaked, her voice off-key, "when a huge warrior grabbed me. He was dressed for the sing-sing. His bracelet cut my face, and he nearly broke my neck when he yanked the chain. My pearl is gone! Oh, William, what will Graham say?"

"He'd better say he's glad to have you and forget the pearl! You could have been killed!"

"How did anyone know I had the pearl?" She couldn't stop crying and was still shuddering at the thought of that horribly painted face thrust so near hers and that rough hand down her dress. William held her close and gently tilted her bruised face up to his. He shook his head. "When are you going to learn to stick with me?"

He helped her to the car, his arms strong and gentle. When he put her into the car, he kissed her bruised, cut face and gave her his wet handkerchief to hold against it. "I'm so sorry. Please forgive me for allowing you to be hurt like this."

He was grim all the way back to Mount Hagen, and they barely noticed that the views from the hilltops were still breathtaking. Julia's face was swelling and turning blue but the bleeding had stopped. They went straight to a doctor's office. The doctor cleaned Julia's wound and said he thought Julie would be all right although there might be a scar on her face.

Then they went to the Mount Hagen police station, abandoning their car and pushing through the crowd of people. They reported the attack and theft. The police were sympathetic when they saw her cut face and swollen lips.

"We'll be lucky if we ever find your pearl, Miss Harrell. Sixty thousand people are jammed into this town, and any one of them could have gone to the bird sanctuary."

"But how did any of the dancers know we were going to the sanctuary? Only Sekiba and the people we stayed with last night knew."

"Perhaps someone overheard us this morning," William suggested. "When we told the people at the rent-a-car place where we were going, there were a good many people standing around."

The policeman said, "Probably the one who did it will simply fade back into his village, and we'll never see that pearl. But let us know if you see the man among the crowd."

Julia shuddered. "I'm not going to watch those painted faces anymore. I've had enough. I'm going to Sydney tomorrow. My fiance lives there, and probably the police from there will be in touch with you." She turned to William. "Let's go, William, I'm exhausted. We've been here at the station nearly two hours."

William was enmeshed in gloom. "Oh, Julie, Julie! I'm so sorry that our last day together had to end like this. I wanted today to be something special we could always remember. Well, I suppose we will remember it! I'll take you back to the house, and you can get some sleep. We fly out very early tomorrow, you know."

"Don't worry, William. All this trouble isn't *your* fault. I wanted to remember our last day together too."

Before taking some tranquilizers so she could sleep, Julia sent a cable to Graham: PEARL STOLEN TODAY. POLICE INFORMED. ARRIVING TAA FLIGHT 1305. 4:55 P.M. FRIDAY. LOVE, JULIA.

The next morning she looked into the mirror and groaned. What a sight to meet her fiance! Graham wouldn't even recognize her. Her face was puffed and blue. The gash on her cheek looked awful. Her mouth was swollen out of shape, and there was a long, ugly red mark on her neck. If she'd wear a veil for a week or so, it would be a good idea, she thought. She couldn't help but giggle, though it hurt her mouth, at a vision of Graham's shock when he had to raise the veil to kiss her. Knowing his fastidiousness, she would probably remain unkissed.

William whistled when he saw her in the early light of dawn. He shook his head. "It's the acid test."

"What's the acid test?" she mumbled.

"If Moresby kisses you when he sees you like that, it's the test of love." So saying, he lifted her clear off the floor and kissed her gently. "I won't say I'm sorry. I had to kiss you just one more time, bruised face or not. Please, Julie, never forget it. *I love you!*" He blinked at the tears in his eyes.

They flew in the usual small Papuan Air Lines plane from Mount Hagen down to Port Moresby, where the large Trans-Australian jet gleamed on the runway. William and Julia were the first to board. As they buckled their seat belts, William voiced a concern. "I wish I knew what happened to Sekiba. Last night when we got to the house from the police station, he was there but—"

"Oh, I forgot all about Sekiba. All I wanted was a bath and a sleeping pill and bed! What happened to him?"

William shook his head. "I don't know. He was there when we got home from the police station. He hung up my jacket for me, and I rested while you took your bath. Later after you'd gone to bed I started to take a shower and realized I had no razor blades. I'd forgotten them. So I sent Sekiba to the bazaar for some new blades. But he didn't come back and I had to borrow a blade from Tom, our host. And this morning Sekiba still hadn't returned."

"He must have stayed to watch more of the sing-sing," Julia suggested.

"But it isn't a bit like him, especially when I'm leaving for two weeks. Surely he should have been back this morning. But then, of course, we had to catch that early plane. He must have met some friends and spent the night with them."

"Well, don't worry about him," she said through puffy lips. It was so hard to talk! "When you get back here after your leave, he will be waiting for you in Bulai."

William looked swiftly at Julia and muttered, "But *you* won't!"

Julia simply couldn't help the tears that rushed to her eyes. But she knew it was only from the shock she'd had yesterday. Her head felt so heavy and her whole face ached. The bruise was a wide, blue streak running from the corner of her mouth, through the gash, and on up to her eye. She leaned back and closed her eyes. "I feel terrible to leave that beautiful pearl behind. Wonder if the police will ever find it."

"They are thorough. Despite what they say, I think they are sure to find it. It will be a tough job though, with so many strange people in town."

"They'll never find it," Julia mourned, rolling her head back and forth against the seat back. "And Graham will think I was careless with it. Just think, it has been in his family since the 1800s and *I* had to be the one to lose it. He will never forgive me! But I have been so aware of it all the time. It was always with me."

William sighed and made a great effort to erase the gloom. "Well, I see I'll have to cheer up the downhearted. Where's my little bamboo flute? Like to hear Mister Banner's famous rendition?"

Julie tried to rally. "Of course. You're a genius with 'Waltzing Matilda.'"

The first five notes came out fine, but he couldn't hit the high note on the second "waltzing." He tried it again, and still the high note sliced off. Finally he quit trying and put the flute back into his pocket. "Everything's going wrong," he muttered. "I lost my girl, she lost her pearl, and now I'm losing my talent. Next I'll probably lose my marbles!"

"You're just not a good 'waltzer.'" She tried to smile but her lips hurt too much. Then she dozed, woke up, tried to eat lunch and dozed again. It was good to have William fussing over her. He asked the stewardess to give him an iced cloth which he held against her cheek, and he asked for some tea when he saw her stirring.

The stewardess looked with concern at Julia's face but said nothing.

Julia giggled. "William, what do you suppose these people think about all my bruises?"

A smile quirked his mouth. "They probably think your husband gave you a beating and now you are running away with your lover!"

Shadows of the great barrier reef and finally Sydney's great harbor appeared below. Their jet soon nosed in for a smooth landing. Julia had not expected Graham outside to meet the plane because she knew all welcoming parties had to stay inside until customs were cleared. But there he was, big, clean-smelling, handsome. His arm enveloped her shoulders as she stepped onto the ramp.

"Julia, what in the world! You are a mass of bruises! I can't take you to any parties for a while! People will think I've been beating you!"

The last thing Julia wanted was a party. She couldn't help the tears that rolled down swollen cheeks. "I'm so sorry about your beautiful pearl, Graham! I'd kept it so carefully hidden all the time we were in Mount Hagen!"

"Don't worry about it, Love. I think it will be found. We've been in touch with the Mount Hagen police already. Hello, isn't this William Banner?"

"Oh, excuse me," she exclaimed. "Yes, Graham, William's furlough was due. The big sing-sing was on in Mount Hagen, and we both wanted to see it. William was with me at the bird sanctuary when the pearl was stolen." That was quite a speech through bruised lips.

"How do you do, Banner?" Graham stuck out his huge hand. "Thanks awfully for looking after Julia for me."

"It was a pleasure. Sorry I didn't do a better job. When she was attacked, I had stopped to get a picture of the cassowaries."

"Well, perhaps there wasn't anything you could have done

anyway. Someone probably knew about the pearl and decided that was the best place to pinch it."

"It was a horrible-looking warrior who attacked me," Julia told Graham. "I'm sure I'd never seen him before. How he could possibly have known about the pearl escapes me. And no one knew we were going to the bird sanctuary except the rent-a-car people."

Graham was steering her into the terminal, William tagging along after them. "Come on, love," Graham urged Julia. "They'll take you through customs quickly; then the police want to ask you a few questions. You too, Banner. They've been in contact with the police in Mount Hagen by radio, but they must get the story from you. It's a formality for the insurance people, you know."

"Right." William's passport and customs papers were in his hand. "Got your customs filled out, Julie?"

They were at the customs counters. She handed her papers to an officer there. On his badge was his name, "Tennant." *I was a tenant once on a horse farm in Kentucky eons ago.*

Officer Tennant looked over her papers. He asked the questions which are asked of every person entering Australia, especially from New Guinea. "Any bamboo, wood, fruit or feathers? Anything to declare, Miss Harrell?"

"Yes," Julia replied. "I have a few mask carvings."

"I'll just take a look, Miss Harrell. Please open your cases."

She must have been still partly in shock because her hands were trembling so that Graham had to open the cases. The officer looked inside. "Well, I'll have to keep these carvings for a few minutes until they are passed by quarantine. Please wait here, Miss Harrell. Next, please."

William handed over his papers.

"Will you open your luggage, please?"

William's keys worked smoothly in the locks.

The officer lifted several articles of clothing from William's luggage and felt along the sides. "Any wood, carvings, fruit or feathers, Sir?"

"No."

"Any bamboo?"

"No."

Julia tried to smile. "Mustn't forget your little tootle, William!"

Officer Tennant's brows raised. "What, Miss?"

William looked calm.

The custom's official looked all business. "Tootle, Miss?"

She looked flustered. "Oh, William, I'm sorry I mentioned it." Then to the officer, "Just a little bamboo flute. He's forgotten about it. He was trying to imitate birds and he was playing 'Waltzing Matilda' on the plane flying home."

The officer held out his hand to William. "May I see it, please?"

William's hand went to his pocket and he handed the flute to Officer Tennant. "Sorry, Officer. I completely forgot about it. Too much has happened in the last two days."

Officer Tennant looked at the flute. It was just a simple piece of bamboo, whittled into a mouthpiece on one end, with the usual holes along the side. The other end was a larger joint of bamboo. "Please wait here," he said.

He took Julia's three wood carvings and the bamboo flute and disappeared through a door marked, "Quarantine."

William drummed on the counter with his fingers. When he saw Graham's arm go around Julia's shoulder, he looked away.

Graham looked down at her. "You look funny with a blue, puffy face. I won't be able to take you to the party we had planned for tomorrow. Lots of people are waiting to invite you to teas, dinners and parties all planned for you."

She was too tired to think about teas, dinners and parties.

Two customs officials appeared. "Would you three kindly step this way?"

They all went into the room marked, "Quarantine." It was

full of police. One quickly stepped to William, and before anyone could understand what was happening, locked William's wrists in handcuffs. William's mouth fell open.

Julia stood completely dumb, watching this strange melodrama.

"You're under arrest, Banner."

"What in the world for? You can't arrest me just for forgetting to declare a little bamboo flute!"

"No," the officer retorted. "We are arresting you for being in possession of and transporting stolen property. You will be formally charged tomorrow."

William's mouth was still open. "But—I didn't—wouldn't—I haven't stolen anything!"

There was silence in the room. Julia was stunned. "I thought some people in New Guinea were crazy, but what's the matter with everybody here? What—what did William steal?"

"Your pearl ring, Miss Harrell. He carried it tucked away inside the joint end of his bamboo flute, cleverly hidden."

For a moment she was speechless. She looked from one to the other and then sputtered, "He did NOT! I don't believe a word of it!"

"Here it is, Miss Harrell." The officer laid the lost pearl ring in her hand.

She stared, unbelieving. "But—but William did NOT do it! I know he didn't. He—" she burst into tears. She had almost said, "He loves me!"

"Come along now," the officer jerked William's wrists none too gently, and another officer ushered William out of the room.

Julia stood sobbing. "Don't put him in jail. I KNOW he didn't steal my ring. There is some mistake!"

One of the policemen spoke gently to her. "Don't be too sure, Miss. We've done a spot of checking on Banner. According to acquaintances, the Banner family has always been more than a little envious of the Moresby family over this pearl. Mr. Moresby said—"

Julia stamped her foot so hard her face hurt. "I don't care what anybody said. I know all about that; William told me about that a long time ago. It doesn't mean a thing. I know William. He did NOT steal my pearl. If he'd wanted it, he could have stolen it any time during the past nine months!"

"Well, we think he hired it done. It was easy to find his servant in Mount Hagen and make him talk. He had been hit by a lorry (truck) and is now in the hospital. We think Banner had his servant hire one of the dancers to get the pearl from you. That's why he took you to the bird sanctuary—there'd be no witnesses."

Julia felt as if *she'd* been hit by a truck. "Sekiba? In the hospital? Hiring a dancer to steal it?" She sounded like an idiot to herself. Her mind flashed back to the bird sanctuary and how tenderly William had held her and carried her. She simply stood shaking her head.

"Anyway," the officer went on, "Banner's servant told the police in Mount Hagen that he paid the warrior two pigs to steal it."

Tears kept rolling down Julia's face as she laughed hysterically. "Two pigs for a pearl like this!" *Could William have planned the whole thing? Is that why he let me walk away from him down the path alone when he pretended to be taking pictures of the cassowaries? No! Absolutely not! That is an outrageous suspicion. He is not guilty! He loves me.* She was laughing and crying at the same time.

Graham took her arm. "Let's go," he said gruffly. "I never did like Banner anyway, not even way back in school. He's got pigs' eyes himself, and I don't like the way he looks at you. Why you ever went to Mount Hagen with him I will never know. Come on, I'll take you to Aunt Rosa's house. You've had enough for one day."

Chapter 12

Julia let Graham lead her away. He first picked up her mask carvings, which were marked, "Passed," and put them back into her suitcase. He was grumbling, "What in the world do you want with those awful looking things? Where will you put them in our home?"

As he guided her out the door, she tottered beside him, utterly bewildered. The whole world had gone crazy. She could barely say hello to Aunt Rosa when she met them at the door.

Aunt Rosa took one look at Julia's distorted face and her hand flew to her open mouth. "Oh, my poor dear! What in the world did they do to you? I knew something terrible would happen to you in that wilderness with all those savages! Come, let me give you something to eat and a cold cloth on your face and help you get to bed—"

She rattled on and on, while hanging up Julia's coat; then she flitted into the kitchen and fussed around with the teapot and the refrigerator. "We must get your poor face well. There are all sorts of dinners and parties planned for you. And there is supposed to be a fitting of your trousseau tomorrow. It's the most divine trousseau I've ever seen. Graham's mother and I planned it all. Oh, you'll make a beautiful bride, Julia, if we can ever get your face healed up. Where is that baked chicken I had in here? Graham, will you stay for some tea with us?"

Graham finally had a chance to say something. "No, Aunt Rosa. I know Julia is tired and has had quite a trying two days—being beaten by a savage, losing the pearl and discovering she's been traveling with a thief. I think she should go to bed. She will have to have several days of rest and recuperation. Our plans will have to wait for a while." He was in complete command of the situation. Turning to Julia he said, "Goodnight, my dear. Sleep well. I'll call you tomorrow." He squeezed her hand, patted her shoulder and left.

She looked dumbly after him. What was that silly thing William had said at dawn today in Mount Hagen about an acid test? Graham had just flunked it! *But I must be crazy to expect him to kiss me when my face looks so awful!*

Aunt Rosa gave her tea in a beautiful Haviland cup. How fragile it was, how exquisite! How different from the plastic cup she'd used for the past two years! Aunt Rosa's tea was soothing; she was so tired.

Aunt Rosa's blue eyes were wide. "What was it Graham said about traveling with a thief? What did he mean?"

"Oh, Aunt Rosa, they have accused William Banner of being a thief and stealing my pearl. I *know* he did not do it. Somehow the pearl got into his bamboo flute, and he brought it in his pocket from New Guinea and the police discovered it. But there's a big mistake. William is *not* a thief! He loves me, Aunt Rosa." Her lips were too swollen to talk so much.

Aunt Rosa's brow puckered and then she must have remembered about wrinkles, for she smoothed it with her fingertips. "Loves you? Well, now, you can never tell, Julia. Perhaps the temptation of having you alone and knowing you had the pearl was just too much. Some men are weak, you know."

"Oh, Aunt Rosa!" Julia could only shake her head. "If you knew William as I know him! He's . . . may I go to bed? I'm exhausted!"

"Of course, my dear. You can sleep tomorrow until you

want to get up. The fittings can wait a few days. Here, let me give you a nightgown. I'll start your bath."

She took from the drawer a filmy, short nightgown of yellow with a peignoir to match. Julia held the bit of froth in her hand for a moment remembering her thick, granny nightgown in Bulai. When she climbed into the deep, warm, fragrant bath, she couldn't help but see the bucket with holes in the cold bathroom in Bulai. She slid way down into the beautiful, scented water, took a deep breath and began to relax. Then tears began spilling down her face, dripping off her chin and salting the bath water. William was in jail because they said he was a thief. How could educated people in Sydney be so stupid?

She gulped down a sleeping pill and crawled thankfully between Aunt Rosa's smooth sheets. Oh, what luxury! Her aching body sank into the soft bed and she was almost asleep, though it was still daylight, when she snapped momentarily awake. The mental picture of William on a hard cot in jail kept coming back. She did the only thing she could—she prayed. "Oh God, please let them find out William isn't guilty. He *isn't!* He believes in you and trusts in you. You know he isn't guilty, Lord."

It was almost noon when Julia awoke the next day. She stretched in bed and tried to go back to sleep, but she was wide awake. So she plopped her feet on the floor and peeked into a large mirror. *Ugh! No wonder Graham didn't kiss me. I can't stand the sight of myself.* Her face had begun to turn a peculiar mixture of purple and yellow.

Aunt Rosa had left a note propped up on the hall table. "Julia, I have a luncheon and an appointment at the hairdresser. Please make yourself at home and *rest.*" The phone rang. It was Graham.

"How are you feeling, darling?"

"Much better. I just woke up. Graham?"

"Yes?"

"Please do what you can to get William out of jail."

"But, Julia, I never take criminal cases."

"William is *not* a criminal, Graham. There has been a big mistake. He did *not* steal this pearl."

"I'm thankful to have it back, love. But we will have to let the law takes its course."

"There isn't *anything* you can do?"

"Not at this juncture."

"Have you checked with the police this morning? Maybe they've found out something new."

"I've checked. Nothing new. Banner will be formally charged today. Don't worry about him, love. You just rest and get your face cleared up. I want to show you off. Well, I have some work waiting so I must go now. I'll come over later this afternoon for a bit. Goodbye, love."

"Bye." She hung up, feeling completely frustrated. *William is still in jail, and I don't believe Graham. I am sure he could help William if he wanted to. He has lots of influence in Sydney.*

Julia wandered around the house. *Why do I have to look so bad? I ought to be out trying on my trousseau. In fact I ought to be excited about it.* But she was restless. Adjustment to Sydney and city life would take some time. There were so many people around, things seemed so crowded. Houses were too close together and traffic was too noisy. Now she understood what William meant when he said that in New Guinea a man could sort out his values and have time to ponder.

William ought to have time to ponder now. He's been in jail more than 20 hours. She had time to ponder, too. She lay back on the couch and began to reflect on the times that were magnified in her mind as important, mirroring them as if they were just happening. *All the times William and I hiked over the hills and talked. At first he said, "I intend to find my pearl or maybe gold." And many times he said he believed in God, and since he believed that, he understood God's demands for his own allegiance. And again—"The goal of getting rich and well-known in Sydney society is gone."*

"Of course he didn't steal my pearl," Julia declared aloud to an empty house. "He didn't even want a pearl anymore. Other things are more important to him."

An inner voice questioned, "What other things?"

I am. He said so a dozen times or more.

Wonder how important I am to Graham. He has asked me to marry him. But he never really listens to me. If he isn't talking, then his mind is wandering somewhere else when I am talking. People like to be near those who will listen to them! But Graham says he loves me and feels I will fit into his life here. Suppose I don't fit in—not quite? Will he love me for what I am? What if he doesn't? I am sure he loves what he feels I will become, not necessarily just what I am now. Graham really doesn't know me very well—not nearly as well as William does.

What is the challenge here for me? Julia had a flash of her future self in a round of social activities—rich, safe and secure and serenely contributing nothing of importance to anyone.

At least in Bulai I had a part in helping some people. There was a personal challenge in it. And I was teaching Megia to read. Why didn't I teach more people? There were others I could have and should have helped. And what about the challenge of the confrontation William spoke of? The confrontation of God for my personal allegiance—giving my life over to Jesus Christ? That has to be reckoned with someday, and I keep putting it off. Why? I don't know. Afraid of what Graham would say, I guess. I know that William has made his choice, and his life is different from when I first met him. Well, since he is God's man, it is up to God to get him out of jail and prove his innocence.

She prowled around Aunt Rosa's house.

Graham came about six o'clock. He hugged her. He was so handsome, so well-dressed, so sure of himself.

"Are you feeling better, love?"

They sat on the couch, and he held her hand in his big one. "I feel all right, but I'm so restless. Are you sure you can't do anything for William?"

"No. If they prove he did it, I may be able to get his sentence lightened if it will please you."

"Not because it will please me, Graham, but because he isn't guilty."

"It's a good trait to be so loyal to your friends, my love, but it looks like the evidence is against him. But don't worry about him, you are safe in Sydney with me now. I'm sorry you had to get into all that trouble. We will have to postpone our wedding for a little while until your face is back to normal. It will take some time to get your trousseau ready too. There are so many things planned for you; my mother is arranging several luncheons and teas."

Julia jumped up and walked to the window. "I have to tell you something, Graham. William is in love with me." There, she'd said it; it was out in the open.

Graham shrugged. "I'm not surprised. I thought possibly he was. Well, I'm sorry for him. Stealing the pearl was a stupid thing to do."

She felt smothered. "Oh, Graham, let's *go* somewhere. Take me for a walk or something! Aunt Rosa's house is beautiful but I feel like *I'm* in prison right now!"

He looked swiftly at her face. "But, love, you can't go out for a few days. Actually, I intended to take you to a dinner party tonight. But you must buy a new dinner gown soon. This party tonight is one I promised to go to a long time ago, so I can't disappoint them. It's an important dinner. I'm so sorry."

"Do you really *have* to go?" She was longing for him to say he would rather stay with her.

He looked at his watch. "Yes, love, I really do have to go. By next week you'll be out—don't fret now." He kissed her forehead, the only spot with no bruises. "Goodbye for now. See you tomorrow."

After his car pulled away, Julia tied a scarf over her head, low so that most of her face was hidden, and plunged out the door. She had to have some fresh air. Oh, for a rocky hillside to walk on!

She walked, knowing no one, speaking to no one, up one paved Sydney street and down another, then close by the sea, where she sat for a long time gazing at the rolling waves. She felt utterly bereft and abandoned. There was an idea—a nebulous, fleeting thought, whirling around like an ice skater on one toe—a conclusion just out of her reach. What was she trying to understand? The future did not glow with happy anticipation for her. Something was wrong. Why was she so depressed? Maybe there was a reason for all this feeling. Why did everything seem so dark?

She suddenly remembered something Marvin had said back in Bulai, the day he'd asked Mary to marry him. *He had said, "If I am troubled, God allows it to teach me something."*

Perhaps in the troubled darkness a person can learn a lesson which will never be forgotten when it is light again!

She jumped up, again striding along the walkways and talking to herself. "Face it, Julia! You are not really in love with Graham Moresby." She gasped and declared aloud again, "I am not in love with Graham Moresby!" She repeated it again. Even as she said it, she felt free. She looked at the beautiful pearl on her finger. Nothing had changed about its lustre, but her feeling for Graham had lost its lustre. *He is handsome, and I admired him. Because he singled me out I was flattered, dazzled by the things he represented: a place in society, entrance into the best places, the finest things. I was enamored by social position and financial security. My feeling for Graham has not been love, but a dazed thankfulness that he would love me. And if he would, things would come to me automatically.*

Wonder if Graham would ever help me babysit some pigs? In his custom-made suit? She laughed to the wind.

She reasoned slowly aloud, "Married to Graham, I would be rich in things with a poverty-stricken soul!"

Graham said yesterday that William had pigs' eyes. *That is unforgivable. He has never seen William's eyes twinkle when William said, "Hi, Red, I love you!" No, he would never see that.*

Suppose they put William in prison for 10 years? An absolutely unthinkable thought!

But suppose they do?

"Then I'll wait!"

The lights of Sydney never twinkled brighter. She walked free. She tore off her head scarf and let her hair blow in the wind. "So what if someone sees my bruises!"

Julia used to watch little colts in the Kentucky bluegrass kicking up their heels just for the sheer joy of living. There on a beach in Sydney, she felt just like that. *I LOVE William! I am in love with William! I know now that William is the one God has chosen for me. How could one person have been so dense for so long? How could it be I never saw it before? How could I have wasted so much time?* She didn't remember touching the ground all the way home.

She ran up the steps into Aunt Rosa's house.

"Oh, Julia, I was worried about you. Where did you go? Oh, your poor face. It's purple today!"

Julia whirled her around, "I'm so happy, Aunt Rosa."

"I'm glad, dear, that you are feeling much better than you did yesterday. Graham will be glad to know."

"I'm starved, Aunt Rosa. May I have some more of that chicken you had yesterday? And some more tea?"

"Of course, help yourself. Frederick is taking me out. Do you like my new hairdo? I had it puffed just a bit more. Frederick thinks it makes me look younger."

"It's lovely, Aunt Rosa." But Julia barely heard her. *I'm in love with William. I'm in love with William! Tomorrow I'm going to the jail and tell him so!* Chicken and tea never tasted better.

Before going to bed she put the pearl ring on the dressing table and got down on her knees beside the bed. Her prayer was first for William, then for herself.

"Oh God, thank you for being so patient with me. Please get William free—we both know he is not a thief. He has committed his life to you—I know that, and I know he isn't guilty.

"And, Lord, I ask you to forgive me for all my sins and selfishness. I've been proud and grasping for fancy things and neglecting the most important things in life. Please, Lord, Jesus, forgive me for that. I want to be a true Christian. I am now committing my life to you. I want your love to fill my heart. Let your Spirit live within me. I do want to live for you. Use me to spread your love in New Guinea like Marvin and Mr. Roper.

"Help Graham not to mourn or feel bad over my breaking this engagement. It never should have been in the first place.

"Oh, Lord, thank you for William's love. Help him to forgive me and help me to be worthy of him. Help us live together in true Christian love for one another. Thank you, thank you, Lord."

As she knelt and prayed, a wonderful warmth pervaded her being. Tears rolled onto the sheet as she prayed and cried in joy. Peace enveloped her as she climbed into bed, no longer needing a sleeping pill. She fell asleep scratching her right foot with her left big toe.

She was startled awake early by the phone. It was Graham. "The police want us to come to the station, love. I'll pick you up in half an hour. Did you get a good sleep?"

"The best in a long time."

"That's fine. Well, this will soon be over."

"I hope so, Graham!"

She put the pearl ring into her purse before going out the door. Graham was, as usual, impeccably dressed. He squeezed her arm in greeting and helped her into his car. "This will soon be all over," he said again.

She nodded but didn't answer and there was no further conversation as they drove to the police station. But she was silently praying, *Please, Lord, let William go free. Help him prove his innocence.*

William was waiting with some officers in a room at the police station as they entered. He was not wearing handcuffs, but he looked grim and unshaven. His brown hair was tousled, and Julia had a great urge to brush it for him. His eyes had a baffled expression. She paused a moment and laid her hand on his arm. "I know you didn't do it, William. No matter what they say, I know!"

He nodded.

The inspector spoke. "Come in and sit down, Miss Harrell, Mr. Moresby. Sit there, Mr. Banner." He shuffled some papers. "We've got further news for you all. Haven't told Banner yet. We've been in radio contact with Mount Hagen police again, and it's a strange story they tell." When they were all seated, he continued. "It seems Banner's servant, Sekiba, thought he would do his master a big favor. He thought his master wanted the pearl so Sekiba decided to get if for him."

Julia gasped.

"Whatever made him think I wanted the thing?" William exploded.

The officer went on. "This is the confession which we got over the wire from the officers in Mount Hagen." The officer began reading from a paper.

Sekiba said: *"One time Mastah speak me him laik pink-misis ring and pink-misis too. Sekiba want Mastah have what him laik. So Sekiba pay sing-sing pella two pigs and say, steal ring from misis. Sekiba put ring in Mastah bamboo. Mastah he no savve. Me like tell Mastah 'bout ring, but Mastah say go get razor blades. Sekiba go, but lorry hit Sekiba, bang!"*

"So that's it," the officer continued. "The police in Mount

Hagen carefully translated the pidgin for me so I got it straight. I'll be glad when they learn proper English!

"Sekiba, because he was such a loyal servant thought that he should get whatever his master wanted. He *thought* Mr. Banner wanted the pearl. So Sekiba hired one of the dancers at the Mount Hagen show to steal the ring. He knew you were going to the bird sanctuary, and he had the dancer follow you somehow. The time you spent in the police station at Mount Hagen gave the dancer an opportunity to deliver the pearl to Sekiba. That evening Sekiba took the bamboo flute out of Banner's pocket and very cleverly opened the end and hid the ring there. He insists that Banner knew absolutely nothing about stealing the pearl. So you have been exonerated, Mr. Banner. You are free. You can go. We are sorry for the inconvenience."

William sagged with relief. He sat breathing deeply, a dazed expression on his face.

Tears rolled down Julia's face—great joy in her heart.

They sat in unbelieving silence; then Julia began to laugh, "Oh, William, no wonder you couldn't hit the high note on 'Waltzing Matilda.' The pearl split your high note!"

William ground his teeth. "When I get back to New Guinea, I'll skin that Sekiba alive!"

The police inspector said slowly, "I don't know about that, Banner. There's more to the report. The police there told us that, because he was hit by a truck, Sekiba is now convinced that what he did was a great sin and that the devil will get him because of it. You know how they believe in spirits. He keeps saying, 'Me gat rong!' and that anybody who does such a big sin deserves to die. In the beginning he thought he was helping you. Now he is sure he will die. Police there say that when a New Guinean thinks the devil is after him he usually *does* die."

"He can't die!" Julia gasped. "He's married now and his wife is going to have a baby in four months!"

William closed his eyes, his head in his hands. "I can't

believe he would be so stupid. But I remember one day when he told me, 'Better go 'long look out. If Dewel say you die, you die, pinish.'"

"But, William," Julia argued, "both he and Megia became Christians and were baptized. Don't you think that would mean he no longer believed that evil spirits could make him die? Don't you think his belief in God is strong?"

William looked bewildered. "I don't know, maybe not strong *enough!*" He shook his head. "Old beliefs and fears die hard, and I'm afraid for him." He raised his head and stood up. "I'm going back now, Julie. I believe I can get there before it's too late. If I can, I'm literally going to command the devil to leave him alone, like Marvin has done sometimes. He'll listen to me." He came over and touched her shoulder. "I've just *got* to have the kind of faith Marvin has for this. Pray that I'll get there in time. Pray for me. Pray for Sekiba!" Then he gently added, "Goodbye, Julie. Be happy." He strode out the door.

"William, wait— I— want to tell you—"

He was gone.

Julia stood in a daze.

Graham said, "Thank you, Inspector. You've been very kind." Then he took Julia's arm and led her outside. William had already disappeared.

Julia was completely stunned. The incidents had all happened so fast, she had a hard time keeping her wits. She suddenly thought of a New Guinean swinging bamboo bridge, suspended between two arched pylons and William stepping out on the bridge alone. But she didn't want William on a swinging bridge in New Guinea or anywhere else without her. He had always said, "Stick with me, Red!"

She turned to Graham in the Sydney sunshine, quickly fished the pearl ring out of her purse and dropped it into his hand.

"Julia! W-what's this?" For once he was flabbergasted!

"I'm sorry, Graham," she said, looking up into his disbelieving eyes. "I was about to make a terrible mistake. I realized last night that I don't really love you. I'm in love with William and didn't know it before. Please forgive me. I have to get to the airport before William leaves!"

"But, Julia, I do love you. Don't be hasty in this decision! Please think about it."

"Graham, you don't really love me either. You don't even know me very well. I'm sure you will agree when you think it through. I'm sorry I don't have more time to talk about it now, but I know God wants me with William. I have to get a taxi to the airport."

"The airport is a long way. I'll drive you."

"No thanks, Graham. I'm sorry—please forgive me." Then ignoring the pain, she pursed her sore lips and whistled a loud, shrill note—the kind she used to whistle to the horses years ago on a Kentucky farm. A passing taxi driver grinned and pulled over.

She climbed into the car. "Goodbye, Graham. I hope you find someone who will make you happier than I ever could." The taxi sped away.

The driver exclaimed, "Not many ladies can whistle like that!" Then he looked at her face in the mirror and shook his head. "You must be some lady!"

She laughed and her lips hurt. "You mean my face? Well, you should have seen the other guy! I don't mean I hit him. I was attacked by a warrior in New Guinea. He was something to look at! He had pigs' tusks stuck in his nose!"

It was the driver's turn to whistle.

The taxi crawled through traffic. When it finally reached the airport she thrust some money into the driver's hand and dashed through one of the double doors of the terminal. A voice on the loudspeaker was announcing, "The TAA flight to Port Moresby, New Guinea, will be boarding at 11:30 through gate 17."

She glanced at the clock. Twenty-five minutes to go. Her heels beat a tattoo across the lobby and up to the ticket counter. She brushed William's arm with her bruised cheek and leaned against him. He smelled like William, only more so—he hadn't bathed in two days.

He looked down in surprise, his hair still tousled, his cheeks shadowed, his eyes bleak.

She looked up, deep into his eyes, and said through swollen lips, "William, ask the man if he can give us *two* tickets back to New Guinea."

A tiny flame lit way back in the brown depths of William's eyes and glowed there. He looked down, way down at Julia's feet. One shoe was off, her toes were wiggling, and she was rubbing the sole of her foot on the buckle of her shoe.

William laughed aloud and his arms went around her— her arms around his neck. "Feet itch?" he asked.

"Like crazy. I hear firecrackers popping too!"

"You mean you're cancelling that big insurance policy, Red?"

"It's already cancelled."

"And you're casting your pearl before swine?"

"It's already cast. Back to pig-sitting!" she said ecstatically.

Then William gloriously passed the acid test. He leaned down and kissed her bruised mouth. His rough beard hurt, but no kiss was ever sweeter.

The airline clerk yawned and waited.

Then William laughed and bought their tickets back to New Guinea. Julia stood scratching her foot and grinning with marshmallow lips while skyrockets exploded all over the place.